LAMECH'S REBELLION

By Ted Merritt

“Do hard things” – Teddy Roosevelt

“Whenever the devil says to me, ‘You’re just one man. You can’t do much, so why do anything?’, I fire back, ‘You’re right, Satan. I can’t do much. But what little I can do, I will do” – Ted Merritt

“Making a few big decisions in life will keep you from having to make a lot of little ones” – Unknown

CONTENTS

Ted Merritt

Eph. 5: 8-11

AUTHOR'S NOTE

For those of you who don't know, this is actually my second published work. My first book, "'Till He Comes: A Look at the Return of Jesus and the End of the World," was released by Amazon on November 14, 2014. Before I ever published it, I made the decision that if I ever wrote a second book that I would correct any significant errors from the first book and put the corrections in the second one. Well, after carefully reading my first book, I found something that may need some clarification.

If you happen to own a copy of 'Till He Comes, and if you purchased it between its release date of November 14, 2014 and April 27, 2015, turn to page 218 and read the last paragraph, which carries over into page 219. Here's how it reads:

> "Do you see there in v. 25, where it says that God provided a propitiation (aka 'reconciliation') 'by His *blood*'? I always cringe a little when I hear someone say that they 'gave their heart to Jesus' or they 'took Jesus into their heart' or they 'received Jesus.' Even Muslims and Buddhists will tip their hat to Jesus, but that doesn't save anybody. In the same way Noah desperately needed a waterproofing agent that would protect him from God's wrath, you and I need something that will protect us. That's where the blood of the Savior comes in."

After having received a little bit of feedback from several people who read the book and seemed confused by my comments here, I realized that this was missing something. As a result, I went back and added the following sentences:

> "When I say that I tend to grimace over someone 'giving their heart to Jesus,' it's because Jesus doesn't want your heart. Seriously, what does a perfect and holy God want with that rotting, putrid thing? No! He wants to give you a *new* heart (cf. Ezek. 36:26)."

This may not be a terribly big deal, but I feel better knowing that my readers have a clear understanding of the gospel. When I hear someone say that they've "taken Jesus into their heart," I know what they're trying to say. That doesn't keep me from being bothered by it, though, because, like I say here, God doesn't really want to send Jesus to live in "your heart." He wants to transform your heart and make you into the likeness of Jesus (Rom. 8:29)!

ACKNOWLEDGEMENTS

"Who can find a virtuous wife? For her worth is far above rubies. The heart of her husband safely trusts her; So he will have no lack of gain. She does him good and not evil All the days of her life. Many daughters have done well, But you excel them all. Charm is deceitful and beauty is passing, But a woman who fears the Lord, she shall be praised. Give her the fruit of her hands, And let her own works praise her in the gates" (Prov. 31:10-12, 29-31).

This is how I would describe the woman God gave to me nearly 30 years ago. Anyone who can put up with me for as long as she has must indeed be a godly person! Without Debbie, there's no telling if I would ever have been able to complete this project. It's easy to thank her for things like her wise words of advice, the grueling task of proofreading and editing, and giving me the occasional kick in the shin I needed to stay focused on my work.

But Debbie does much more than that. She makes our home a comfortable and welcoming place. She comes in behind me and throws out (or gives away) all the pointless junk I try to collect. She spoils me with the best country cooking in the South. She reads to me at bedtime, she hugs me when I'm sad, she calms me when I'm afraid, she helps me understand the hardest things in life, she makes me laugh like no one else can. She is my best friend. She is more beautiful and more precious to me with every passing day. I wish I had the right words to say how much I love her and how much she means to me. Try as I might, the best I can come up with is "Thank you. Your worth is far above rubies."

Thanks also go out to the wonderful people at Southgate Baptist Church, especially our "Big Fat Sunday School Class." Your prayers, encouragement, kindness and friendship mean so very much to Deb and me.

I am also greatly indebted to Chuck Korte for letting me print his wonderful testimony, which he wrote and gave at his baptism. (There wasn't a dry eye in the house at that event!)

Naturally, I give all praise and honor to our great God and Savior Jesus Christ. He is above all things and before all things. One day, He will descend from heaven with a shout, with the voice of an archangel, and with the trumpet of God. Then the saints of God shall be caught up together in the clouds and meet the Lord in the air, and thus we shall always be with the Lord. I can't wait!

Soli Deo Gloria!

INTRODUCTION

"Then Lamech took for himself two wives: the name of one was Adah, and the name of the second was Zillah" – Gen. 4:19.

I never thought I'd write a book that started with a verse like this. But God is highly economical in His use of words, which is to say that every last stroke of His pen is pregnant with meaning. As I considered this strange sentence about a little-known man, I began to realize that God has some important things to say, things that have been relevant for every society in every era since the Fall in Eden.

Lamech, you see, was the seventh generation from Adam through the line of Cain. After Cain murdered his brother Abel, God replaced the lost sibling with another son of Adam; his name was Seth. Now we skip ahead a few years. The tenth generation from Adam (through Seth's line) was a man called Noah. The lineage of all generations alive today travel back through both Noah and Seth and they end with Adam. Cain produced the other line that came from Adam, but all of his descendants died in the great Flood. In spite of the fact that the lamp of Cain was extinguished long ago, there is much that we can learn from him and his progeny.

As a result of Cain's crime, God cursed him and made him live as a fugitive for the rest of his days (Gen. 4:12). When Cain pleaded with God, saying that his punishment was too severe, God showed him mercy by promising that he would be protected from any would-be assailants. In fact, God promised Cain that anyone who dared kill him would be avenged sevenfold (vs. 13-15).

Cain departed from his God and his home, and he took up residence in a foreign land. In the verses leading up to this first statement about Lamech, there is a quick rundown of the sons born into Cain's family tree. Very little is said about the men between Cain and his great-great-great grandson Methushael, but after Methushael comes Lamech, and there are seven verses devoted to him (Gen. 18-24).

As we saw in Gen. 4:19, the first thing we learn about Lamech is that he took two wives. Have you ever stopped to think about what other people say about you when you're not around? Have you given any thought to what might be the most commonly discussed subject when the topic of conversation is you? For Lamech, it was that he "took for himself two wives." I'm quite certain that this wasn't intended to be a compliment. As a matter of fact, nothing in Scripture can be construed as a positive statement about Lamech. In Gen. 4:20-22, Lamech has a few children that left a mark on society, but Lamech's big claim to fame was that he took two wives.

That is in itself a legacy, but being the trailblazer of bigamy cannot in any sense be considered something to crow about. Genesis 2:24 lays down the blueprint for the home:

it is one man and one woman, married for life. Surely Lamech had to notice that neither his fathers before him nor his contemporaries around him had a second spouse. It is therefore not even remotely possible that Lamech acted in ignorance when he stood at the altar a second time (while the first wife looked on). But that didn't stop him. Lamech was absolutely committed to doing what he wanted to do. He didn't care what God said, and he didn't care what society said. The only thing that mattered to Lamech was that he wanted two wives, and that was that.

Somewhere between Lamech's second trip down the aisle and his death, he got hurt in some kind of altercation. In verses 23-24, Lamech told his wives that a young man had wounded him, but they need not fret because he had everything under control. What did Lamech do to remedy the problem? He killed his adversary. It appears that he's attempting to comfort his wives, because in v. 24 he makes the bold prediction that if Grandpa Cain was going to be avenged sevenfold, then he would be avenged seventy-sevenfold.

A couple of things jump out at me here. First, Lamech is following in the footsteps of his great-great-great granddaddy. Got a problem with somebody? Ain't nothin' a little violence can't fix. Cain evidently passed on to his children the notion that you don't need God for anything. If you get crossways with a man, you can take care of it yourself. That was Cain's methodology with his own brother, and he handed this philosophy down to Lamech.

Second, how is Lamech able to make such a wild deduction? It's bad enough that Lamech thought he would receive eleven times more help from God than Cain was promised. What takes Lamech's presumptuous remark into orbit is the fact that he doesn't even know God! The first noteworthy act of his life was that he violated God's plan for marriage. Then, sometime later, he took matters into his own hands and murdered another man, a man who was created in God's image. Lamech certainly showed a lot of gall, didn't he? He actually believed that God was going to be on his side!

On February 7, 2015, I was in the Wal-Mart near my home. I saw a man – a very big man – wearing a T-shirt that had on the back an advertisement for some kind of testosterone replacement or enhancement or something. On the front of his shirt, in huge block letters, it read: FIGHTING SOLVES EVERYTHING. By the way, the guy had his arm in a sling. I wanted to stop him and ask him, "How well does your creed work for you?"

The line of Cain came to an abrupt halt at the Flood, but his legacy lives on. It's nice that Lamech's sons did some good things. One son, Jabal, was the progenitor of nomads who made their living as herdsmen. Jubal, his brother, was "instrumental" in the invention of stringed and wind instruments (pun intended). They had a half-brother, Tubal-Cain, who was the father of metallurgy.

As I said, the creative and truly useful contributions these men made were very nice indeed. It's too bad that their biographies stopped there. These three sons of Lamech, after being introduced in Gen. 4:20-22, never appear in Scripture again. Sadly, neither is Lamech. His story ends in v. 24, where we read of his outlandish boast that God will protect him far beyond what He did for the wicked Cain. (Genesis 5 acquaints us with another man named Lamech, but he was born in the line of Seth. Every subsequent mention of a Lamech in the Bible is in reference to the Lamech of Chapter 5. This second Lamech, by the way, was the father of Noah.)

The Lamech of Chapter 4, though, leaves this world having cast only a temporal, worldly die. Such is not the case with Cain's younger brother. Genesis 4:25 talks of the birth of Seth, and in v. 26 an amazing thing happens: "And as for Seth, to him also a son was born; and he named him Enosh. <u>Then men began to call on the name of the Lord</u>" (emphasis mine). Seth fathered a son, and shortly thereafter man began to be reconciled to his Creator.

Noah was the tenth generation after Adam (and the ninth after Seth). Some 56 generations after Noah, the Messiah was born. That's right, Jesus' heritage can be traced all the way back to Adam through Seth (see Luke 3:23-38). Lamech may be credited with being the father of things having to do with money, music, and metals, but Seth accomplished something infinitely greater: he was the father of many who would come to know the Lord.

The purpose of this book is to figure out what went wrong with Lamech; his errant thinking led him down the path to destruction. My goal is to help you understand the origin, nature, severity, and ultimate results of Lamech's sins. Prov. 19:25a says: "Strike a scoffer, and the simple will become wary..." Lamech was a scoffer. May God grant us the ability to learn from his errors, and that we might not follow in his steps.

PART ONE

WORSHIPING THE CREATURE

"For the wrath of God is revealed from heaven against all ungodliness and unrighteousness of men, who suppress the truth in unrighteousness, because what may be known of God is manifest in them, for God has shown it to them. For since the creation of the world His invisible attributes are clearly seen, being understood by the things that are made, even His eternal power and Godhead, so that they are without excuse, because, although they knew God, they did not glorify Him as God, nor were thankful, but became futile in their thoughts, and their foolish hearts were darkened. Professing to be wise, they became fools, and changed the glory of the incorruptible God into an image made like corruptible man – and birds and four-footed animals and creeping things. Therefore God also gave them up to uncleanness, in the lusts of their hearts, to dishonor their bodies among themselves, who exchanged the truth of God for the lie, and worshiped and served the creature rather than the Creator, who is blessed forever. Amen" – Romans 1:18-25

1

A SIN IS BORN

I once heard a preacher say something very wise. He said, "Making a few big decisions in life will keep you from having to make a lot of little ones." Lamech lived out his life by the seat of his pants. No doubt about it, Lamech didn't just wake up one morning and find two women in his bed. Like all sins committed by all sinners, there is a series of events that lead up to the climactic iniquitous act. James 1:14-15 explains that we are "drawn away" (i.e. led astray) by our desires, which in turn leads to our being enticed. In other words, passing thoughts give rise to titillating contemplation. When that happens, desire is increased. We all know what takes place after that, don't we? We move from casual fleeting thought to deliberate fixation. From there, we graduate to making a plan to commit a sin. Verse 15 says that our desires are like an embryo that develops over time and one day ends in the birth of a sinful action.

What Lamech did to end up with two wives, we're not told. But if you consider the ramifications of Gen. 5:26, it was the line of Seth that is credited with having sought the Lord. It's just another way of saying that Lamech, like his fathers before him and his sons who followed, never cried out to God in repentance or faith.

Make no mistake here. Lamech married a second woman one day, but it didn't "just happen." Lamech knew that God existed, but he was not the slightest bit interested in having a relationship with his Creator. He had heard the stories about Great Grandpa Cain and how God promised to protect him after he murdered his brother, but nothing else about God impressed Lamech. He never bothered to find out what God thought about Cain's sin. If he had, he would've given heed to God's punishment of Cain rather than the safeguard God graciously gave this undeserving sinner.

Do you know anyone like that? Have you ever met a man who was quick to claim God's promises but never paid any attention to what God demands? Have you ever known anyone who took promises from the Bible that were obviously meant for someone else and applied it to themselves? If you know someone like that, then you probably also know someone who also misunderstood God's intentions. Not only did this person take a promise from the Bible and wrongly claim it as his own, but he probably also misunderstood the promise altogether. And when he did that, the story's ending was not a happy one.

That's Lamech. He took a promise from a God he didn't love that was given to a man he didn't know and had stipulations he didn't consider, and in the end he was destroyed in a manner he didn't predict. I don't know how long or how far Lamech had fallen before he ended up with something as rebellious as an adulterous lifestyle, but I do know at least two things. First, Lamech's rebellion came long before he married even the first wife, because he was never one to have called upon the Lord. And second, he never stopped long enough to make the big but simple decision to seek after God. Instead, he made one little decision after another, and it's how he lived his life all the way to its sad and bitter end. Lamech traded a relationship with God for the passing pleasures of this world, and finally the day came when a great Flood came and swept all memory of Lamech and his accomplishments completely away.

2

A DARK EXCHANGE

Go back and read Rom. 1:18-25 again. Better yet, read it four or five times. It will be a tremendous help in getting the words to gel in your mind. Once you've read it several times, go back and look at vs. 18-19 again. You will see there that God's wrath is let loose against unrighteousness because unrighteous people will conceal the truth rather than uphold it and proclaim it. You will also notice that God expects us to know certain things about Him, namely that He exists and that He has shown us His power and might just in the creation itself (which is what we learn in vs. 20-21).

It is here that we find where Lamech fell off the horse. He knew perfectly well that he was wandering into dangerous territory when he did something that no one had ever done before. Lamech never had the written Word of God, but he had to have known that bringing a second woman into his bed was a no-no. It was no accident that none of his forebears had ever veered off into polygamy. I want to pause here and make a couple of important points. First, no one ever stumbled onto a godly lifestyle. The reason that humanity went for a half dozen generations without having committed this sin is because it was a learned behavior. It's plain that God started the world with just one man and one woman, and the fact that Lamech was the first man to venture into this new kind of sin makes for a strong case that Adam and Eve taught all their children this essential principle of monogamy.

Second, this scenario flies in the face of the popular but erroneous belief that the Bible is not clear in anything it means to say. The so-called “emergent church” is rapidly gaining converts to the idea that we can’t know what the Bible really means, which is a backdoor way of trying to make all things permissible. In reality, the Bible is very clear. The problem is not the clarity of the Bible; the problem is that sinful man does not like what the Bible says. The notion that God has not clearly and explicitly told mankind what He expects of us is patently false.

I am well aware that the Bible tackles a host of subjects that are sometimes difficult to grasp, but let there be no doubt that when it comes to life’s most important matters, God has explained Himself with perfect clarity. To take this point another step further, God has every right to demand a reasonable expectation of understanding, belief, and obedience from human beings. We know this to be true because of what I said at the beginning of this chapter about v. 20, that God’s attributes are known to all through creation alone. The universe’s testimony is so compelling that its mere existence takes away our ability to successfully deny the existence of a Creator.

Lamech's sin found a home in his sexuality, but his sinfulness in this arena was the *result* of his defiance of God, not the cause of it. Put another way, Lamech was guilty of idolatry before he was guilty of infidelity. (We will most definitely exhaust Lamech's sexual crimes later in this book, but it's my desire to examine his transgressions in the order that they occurred.) Can you see how Lamech was caught up in this pagan practice of idol worship? It is because he put himself above God. He adored a second woman, but we need to face the fact that he loved her only for what she could give him. He didn't need her to produce offspring for him; his first wife had already done that. The reason for Lamech's unprecedented act was that he determined to have the affections of more than one woman. Is that a sexual sin? Of course it is! But it is first and foremost the sin of idolatry, where Lamech placed his own wants above both God and his two wives. Lamech was acutely interested in giving all worship and praise to *himself*.

Lamech didn't build a statue. He didn't bow down in front of a pagan's altar. What he did do, though, was mix together a potent blend of various evil actions that cemented his fate before a holy God. Just go down the list you're given in vs. 21-23. Lamech knew enough about God to invoke His Name, but he refused to give God glory. In his own unique and thankless manner, Lamech foolishly tried to take what God had given to someone else, and he did it while simultaneously kicking God off His throne (figuratively speaking, of course) and plopping himself down on it.

The daring trade Lamech made reaped its reward in vs. 24-25. God gave Lamech over to his vile lusts, which in turn allowed him to wrongly (and I might add perilously) conclude that he was somehow in the fold of the Lord's protective hedge. You know, there is one thing that's worse than not being a Christian, and that's mistakenly thinking that you are one. Once again, another facet of Lamech's ugly portrait is now made visible to us.

3

WORSHIP AT THE FIRST CHURCH OF LAMECH

Only God knows when Lamech got his chariot off course and ended up in the ditch. All of us, at one time or another, find ourselves outside of God's will. It just happens. It happens because we're all sinners. But God restores His sheep. It's what He did with Jacob. He did it with Moses. He did it with Elijah. He did it with Abraham, and He did it with David. He even restored Peter. That is not so with the man we're studying. Lamech never wanted any part of God's restoration, forgiveness, or even His salvation. All Lamech wanted from God is what God had to offer him right this second, and he didn't want to pay anything for it.

Have you ever heard anyone say that you can have your "best life" right now? For the Christian, that is an outright lie. Over the years, I've developed several mottos, or creeds, that I live by. Here's a sampling: God owns it all. Life is not fair. The House always wins. (That's one that gamblers ought to remember.) Here's a little four-word axiom I came up with a while back, and it's one that Lamech never learned: There are no shortcuts. Nothing truly great ever came easy. Being a great spouse takes a lifetime of hard work. Being a great parent requires the same kind of commitment. It's also true for anyone who aspires to be a great musician, scientist, athlete, doctor, pilot, or scholar.

Lamech never learned this principle. He's like that friend who's always there for you whenever he needs you. He's standing with an outstretched hand, just waiting for God to fill it up with every good thing. God is most assuredly the giver of every good gift (James 1:17), and there is nothing that any man can "do" to earn God's favor. But there is one thing God does demand; we are to have a *relationship* with Him. Lamech wanted no part of that! In regard to women, he was gonna marry whoever he wanted and however many he wanted. When it came to Lamech and his enemies, he was going to kill anybody who might be a bother to him. Lamech devotes his whole life to debauchery, and then he swaggers up to God and says, "I'm a good guy. I work hard for what's mine. All right now, God, You just pour out them blessings, 'cause I'm right here and ready to receive 'em!"

Lamech was no atheist. He didn't try to deny God's existence. On the contrary, he seemed to think that he had it in pretty good with Yahweh. In many ways, though, Lamech was worse than an atheist. This may be a tough pill to swallow, but God actually respects the atheist more than He respects somebody like Lamech. The apostle Paul wrote that "...if anyone does not provide for his own, and especially for those of his household, he has denied the faith and is worse than an unbeliever" (I Tim. 5:8). God says that a sedulous lost man outranks a saved lazy man. This is bad news for Lamech, as he is the poster boy for idleness, which piles insult upon injury since he's unregenerate, too. He preferred killing a man over making a tiny little effort to try and reconcile with him. Then, as if that weren't enough, Lamech thought he could force God's hand and demand that he be protected from the consequences of his sin.

Living a godly life is hard because God's way is almost never the path of least resistance. Lamech, however, was forever bent on trying to find the easy way out. Rather than try to control his baser urges, he succumbed to temptation and brought another woman into his bedroom. Instead of striving to work things out with his enemy, he permanently eliminated the threat. And then, to top it all off, he expected God to smile on him. In I Cor. 9:24-27, Paul exhorts us to work tirelessly to keep our bodies under control. But once again, Lamech spent his years doing the exact opposite.

If you put all this information about Lamech into one big bundle and toss it in the mixing bowl, what comes out is the picture of judgment painted in Romans 1. Verse 21 talks of a man who knew God, which is an abbreviated way of saying that he knew who God was, but nothing more. Lamech knew *of* God, but he had no ambition to cultivate a relationship *with* God. Because he was ungrateful to

God, and because he tried to take advantage of God's goodness, his foolish heart was darkened. When Lamech announced that God somehow owed it to him to protect him, he was claiming to be wise but was only showing himself to be a fool (v. 22). As a result, the Lord turned Lamech over to his own lusts (v. 24), which would someday climax in Lamech's undoing.

There were many elements of Lamech's life that were pieced together to produce the sad condition described in v. 25. He had long ago traded the truth of God for a lie, which slowly but steadily drew him further away from the Creator until he found himself worshiping at the Altar of Lamech. He finally arrived at the place where the most important person in his world was himself. It's a sad and lonely place for anyone to be, but for Lamech, his misery had only just begun.

4

THE NIGHT THE LIGHT WENT OUT

Weird things start to happen to a man when he becomes his own god. His thinking gets clouded, so much so that his life worsens with every passing decision. It's long been an observation of mine that most government agencies, sizable companies, and powerful people have something in common. Whenever they make an error in judgment or bad decision, they almost always follow it up with an even bigger one.

That's essentially what our passage in Romans 1 is saying. The principles it teaches can be applied equally to individual persons as well as whole societies. According to v. 21, all people know God. With that fact as its starting point, we can accurately deduce that it is a part of the sinful nature to take that first step in the wrong direction by refusing to give glory to their Creator. Because of their ingratitude, people's entire mindsets become "darkened." The Greek word here is "skotizo," and it means "to obscure; to cover with darkness; to be deprived of light." It's not just the mind losing its sensitivity to light (or knowledge); God is actively intervening and *preventing* people from receiving the light.

Jesus explained how this phenomenon plays out. In Matthew 13, He teaches His followers using several parables. Following the parable of the sower (vs. 3-9), the disciples ask the Lord why He often relies on parables to teach them. His answer is helpful to us: "He answered and said to them, 'Because it has been given to you to know the mysteries of the kingdom of heaven, but to them it has not been given. For whoever has, to him more will be given, and he will have abundance; but whoever does not have, even what he has will be taken away from him. Therefore I speak to them in parables, because seeing they do not see, and hearing they do not hear, nor do they understand" (Matt. 13:11-13).

In short, people who use the light they're given to seek the Lord will be given more light, but those who reject the light will have it taken from them so that they might live in darkness. A hotly debated subject, usually brought against Christians by skeptics, is the notion that God is not "fair." Many an antagonist has tried to justify his hatred for God by asking questions like this: "You say that your God is a loving God, but you also say that Jesus is the only way to heaven. How do you explain an all-loving God that's willing to send people to hell even though they were never given the chance to hear about Jesus?"

I have many answers to this assault, but I'll take time to give you only a few. First, God does not take pleasure in sending people to hell (II Pet. 3:9). Second, God is completely and perfectly just, so He will punish those who go to hell in a manner that is totally consistent with the amount of information they were given during their time on earth (Luke 12: 47-48). Third, the problem is not that people don't have any knowledge of God. The problem is that they don't *want* to know God. John 3:19 is an excellent summation of this truth: "And this is the condemnation, that the light has come into the world, and men loved darkness rather than light, because their deeds were evil."

The third point leads us directly back to our passage in Romans 1, where it says in vs. 19-20 that the visible world that can be seen by all men is ample proof that there is a God. That proof is so ironclad and so airtight that no one has an excuse to deny God. Now we've come full circle. God gives us two kinds of revelation, general and special. General revelation is the world around us, which is available to everyone and is more than adequate to condemn everyone who rejects it (cf. Tit. 2:11). Special revelation is the Word of God, and though it has not been made available to everyone, the idea is that general revelation is sufficient to give all men the desire to seek God.

The problem with man, however, is that we take the information God gives us and we run in the opposite direction as fast and as far as we can. Why? Because our deeds are evil, and we like it that way! Luke 12:48 makes it clear that a person's eternal punishment will be commensurate with the amount of light (revelation) he has been given but chosen to reject. This is the starting line for all who end up in everlasting hellfire. Whenever the light of truth is shined upon the unregenerate sinner, his first inclination is to turn away from the light and head for the cloaking protection of the dark.

The unsaved soul takes refuge in the darkness. He can't see his sinfulness in the dark. He can't see that God is his enemy while he's hiding in the dark. Here, in the blackness of this cave, he is deceived into thinking that he won't be held accountable to his Creator. A man with a darkened mind and a darkened heart dwelling in a world without light has woven a sticky web for himself; it is the web of unremitting ignorance. He has fooled himself into believing that if he can shut out the truth of God, and if he can somehow achieve this feat for all his days, then God will be unable to convict him on Judgment Day.

Romans 1:20-21 describes the point of origin for every unconverted soul. He has been given more than enough information to know that he should seek out his Maker, but he has refused to accept both the knowledge as well as the God behind that knowledge. From there, he begins his descent toward hell (what Jesus calls the broad road that leads to destruction – Matt. 7:13-14). As we learned from Lamech, the unsaved man does not hold his place in one position for any length of time. Once a person has taken Jesus as his Savior and Lord, he has been put on a course that will expose him to more light (truth) and give him greater knowledge and wisdom about his Master. Conversely, the unredeemed man – the one who turned away from the light – will continue on a path that will put him into greater and deeper darkness.

Not content to worship God, but still possessing a feverish desire to worship someone or something, this lost one will trade the glory of God for an idol of his own making (v. 23). As a result, God will remove the lamp of truth, which will cause this obstinate renegade to live out his days in hedonism, seeking to satisfy an insatiable thirst and become a slave to his every impulse. He will lose his ability to restrain himself with steadily increasing intensity, and he will likewise lose his integrity and self-control. It is at this point that he finds a new god to worship. It may be someone or something else at the outset, but at some point he'll look inward and worship only himself. (As Debbie was editing, she came across this paragraph and asked a rhetorical question: "Doesn't this sound like another man we know? Doesn't this sound just like King Solomon?")

Have you noticed that we've turned a corner? We started our time together by looking at Lamech, one of history's earliest idolaters. But we're not talking about Lamech right now. Don't worry, because we'll get back to him soon enough. There is still much to be learned from this ancient man. For now, though, I want to carry the things we've seen in Lamech into a more modern setting. What

Lamech has taught by his example can be used to help us understand not only ourselves as individuals, but also the entirety of the world around us. If you back up to Rom. 1:18, you will see that what we've been discussing in this book is the early stages of God's judgment being poured out upon a people in revolt against Him. America has fallen lockstep behind Lamech and begun our slide toward utter ruin.

The verses we'll be examining for the remainder of this book will show the chronology of God's timetable of judgment. It should be obvious that our nation is somewhere on this continuum of God's wrath. This means that it would behoove us to find out how far gone we are, and what (if anything) can be done to turn away from the darkness and back in the direction of the life-giving light.

5

LOSING OUR FOCUS

There's a reason why God commands us to put on our "full armor" (Eph. 6:10-18). In this life, in these sinful bodies of ours, we are all in a fight to the finish against evil. I know that I tend to lose my focus in the heat of battle, because the fighting is constant; it never lets up. When I lose my concentration, the first casualty in the camp is me. That's because I get pigheaded and start to reinterpret God's orders. I get the idea that God wants me to find fault with others. Sometimes the word "others" can be translated to mean "the whole world." However, God wants me to understand that the war I'm in is not with the world. After all, God has overcome the world (John 16:33)!

It's true that as a warrior for the Lord, I am expected to stand fast against all the evils this sin-sick planet can throw at me. But that is not the arena where my energies are to be expended. No, the theater to which I've been called is for me, for my survival against the Evil One. It's my duty to recognize that my beloved country is under God's judgment, and I ought to understand its symptoms (cf. I Chr. 12:32; Matt. 16:1-3; Luke 12:54-56). The aim of this, though, is not so I can fix the world around me. Rather, it's so I'll stay on my toes and remain in combat against the tantalizing pull of the world. It's not that I'm supposed to change the world nearly so much as it is that I am to prevent the world from changing me. (We will see this doctrine play out over and over again throughout the book.)

With all this in mind, go back to Romans 1. Just as Lamech's worship began to swerve in the wrong direction, so has ours. Instead of giving all honor and praise to our Maker, we have corrupted our worship by turning toward ourselves. Over the next several chapters, I will show you what this perverted worship looks like.

6

GOIN' GREEN WITH GORE

"The United States and the Soviet Union are mounting large-scale investigations to determine why the Arctic climate is becoming more frigid, why parts of the Arctic sea ice have recently become ominously thicker and whether the extent of that ice cover contributes to the onset of ice ages."[1] So says a New York Times article in the July 18, 1970 edition, which was written by columnist Walter Sullivan. A couple of years later, on September 9, 1972, The Windsor Star (a Canadian newspaper) warned that Planet Earth is on a path toward another ice age. Quoting Prof. Hubert Lamb, director of climate research at a British university, the article laid out its case that man must brace for a bleak and frosty future.

Noting that global temperatures had been steadily declining over the previous twenty years, Lamb declared that "we are on a definite downhill course for the next two centuries... The last 20 years of this century will be progressively colder. After that the climate may warm up again but only for a short period of decades." The article concluded with the observation Lamb made that "...climate changes come in cycles determined by astronomical and physical factors. He said one main cause is the amount of radiation received from the sun."[2]

Fast-forward two more years, to August 8, 1974, where again the New York Times reasserted its doomsday prediction with another ice age forecast with this comment: "The mean temperature of the northern hemisphere increased steadily from the early nineteen-hundreds through the early nineteen-forties. Since then, it has been on its way downward toward the colder circumstances of the last century. The drop since the nineteen-forties has only been about half a degree, but some scientists believe this is enough to trigger changes that could have important effects on the world's weather and agriculture."[3] Then, on November 30, 1976, the Times announced that Columbia University scientist James Hays made this gloomy prediction: "If you project the relationship between the orbits and the climate in the future, this cooling trend should continue for on the order of 20,000 years. In that length of time I think there is not much doubt that we will build substantial ice on the Northern Hemisphere continents."[4]

As I searched the internet for Chicken Little weather predictions made by "experts" during the 1960s and 70s, I found a seemingly infinite number of scientists and climatologists lining up to foment mass hysteria over plummeting global temperatures looming on the horizon. However, it took less than three decades for the meteorological community to completely reverse itself, because now – as everybody knows – it is high time we all start losing our collective heads over the global convection oven that we're in the midst of manufacturing.

In 2006, former Vice President Al Gore published "An Inconvenient Truth," a book that sounded the alarm warning the world that advanced societies (particularly the U.S.) are going to be the cause of weather-related catastrophes. It is well worth mentioning that the book has this catchy subtitle: "The Planetary Emergency of Global Warming and What We Can Do About It." Since the environmentalists from the late twentieth century were proven wrong when an ice age failed to materialize, they had to back up and regroup. They retooled their strategy, and the result was the unveiling of the new and improved disaster known as global warming.

Once again, though, our weather patterns have refused to cooperate, and less than a decade after Gore's foolish work was thrust upon us, these poor folks have had to change their tune once again. Today, we no longer worry about an ice age, and "global warming" is not what it was cracked up to be. The proper term to instill fear in the hearts of men is now the dreaded "climate change."

Perhaps Mr. Gore would garner a little more credibility if he didn't reside in a 10,000-square-foot mansion that gobbles up far more energy than the average American home. According to CBS News, Gore's Nashville house used more than twelve times the city's average single-dwelling residence in 2006, the year his book was released.[5] Let me give you a gentle reminder here. It is not a sin to be rich. It's not even a sin to enjoy all of the comforts and luxuries your bank account will allow. What's sinful is to live in opulence and then make merchandise of the bald-faced lie that the rest of America is guilty of bringing mankind to the brink of extinction because we're all too wasteful and ostentatious.

Whether we're talking about global cooling, global warming, or the advantageously vague problem of "climate change," there is one common thread running through each of these theories. They all suggest that the biggest threat that our world faces is mankind. Is that really the case? Is the human race the premier menace to the continuation of the planet?

7

I KNOW WHOM I HAVE BELIEVED

Lamech thought highly of himself. As his love for self increased, any semblance of his concern for the things of God went by the wayside. This enabled him to come to the wrong conclusion that God would continue to bless him, no matter how self-indulgent he became. Lamech's thinking became progressively more clouded, and he began to see himself as more important than he was.

This is just one of several gaping holes in the thinking behind the environmental movement. The Al Gores of the world assign abilities to man that he does not have. I am unwilling to go along with the faulty belief that man is an unwanted intruder, that the earth would somehow be better off without us. Consider Gen. 1:26 and 9:2, where God plainly says that man is to be the ruler over all creation. In Psalm 8:6-8, David wrote that God gave man responsibility and control over the entire animal kingdom.

When man gets a little too full of himself, he begins to develop an overinflated sense of self-importance. He starts to take his eyes off the Lord, and thoughts form in his mind that he – not God – is in charge. From there, his errors start to compound. If man is in absolute authority, then man has it within his power to either perpetuate the world or utterly obliterate it. This kind of thinking leaves out the God who made and sustains our entire universe. If the environmentalist mentality were correct, man could wrest the throne of the earth away from the One who made it.

Right after the Flood, God spoke to Noah and his sons. In Gen. 9:8-10, the Lord declares that He is making a covenant with both man and beast, which He articulates in the next verse: "Thus I establish My covenant with you: Never again shall all flesh be cut off by the waters of the flood; never again shall there be a flood to destroy the earth" (Gen. 9:11). God repeats this promise more than 1,500 years later, in Isaiah 54:9, where He compares His oath to Noah with a promise to the Jewish people that He would not be angry with them forever, which is another way of saying that He'll always keep His promise to the Jews.

God is 100% at odds with the environmentalist. Either there will be another worldwide flood or there won't, but it has to be one or the other. God never changes, but man's plans and ideas are constantly evolving. That's why there's never been a "Biblegate," but there was most definitely a "Climategate." (There is considerable information available on the internet about this scandal.) The war over man's role in planetary degradation continues to rage. Meanwhile, God's Word has never changed, and it never will.

One really has to stop and ask himself, "What if secular science is right? What if we're on the precipice of causing self-extinction? What then?" Here's my thought pattern. If the secularists are correct, then it makes no difference what we do with our time on earth. Life is utterly meaningless, since all we have to look forward to after this is all over is an eternity filled to the brim with *nothing*. If the so-called naturalists are right, then I have no reason to worry about my own children, much less the fragile habitat of the peacock spider.[1] What difference does it make how many kids I have or what kind of world I pass down to them if they're bound for the exact same empty fate that I must soon meet?

In the case of Naturalist vs. God, the decision comes down to one simple question: Who are you going to believe? Do you believe the fickle, frightened, faltering phonies who are constantly revising and modifying their fault-filled, fallacious findings? Or have you put your trust in the everlasting God, who never changes? Thus says the Lord: "While the earth remains, Seedtime and harvest, Cold and heat, Winter and summer, And day and night Shall not cease" (Gen. 8:22).

8

GREATER THAN A WOMBAT

I made the passing comment in Chapter 7 that I refuse to accept the doctrine that man is an unwelcome trespasser in this accidental universe. By sharp contrast, God says that man is the most important creature of all (in addition to the fact that the universe was by no means an "accident"). One of the earliest methods God used to demonstrate man's exalted position was when He set up the Old Testament system of sacrifice, which called for the slaughtering of animals twice a day every single day in order to maintain a relationship between sinful men and a holy God (cf. Exod. 29:38-42). About 1,500 years after instituting the temple sacrifice, God did the unthinkable by becoming a man and replacing the killing of animals with the offering of Himself. God is supremely concerned about His relationship with man. In Luke 6:6-7, Jesus explains that one person is worth far more than a whole flock of birds. To say that people are no more important than <u>any</u> animal is blasphemy!

Do you think that's too strong of a word? Am I going too far when I say that the environmentalist is a "blasphemer"? Before you say yes, consider a few facts. First, we need to define the word "blasphemy." According to America's greatest dictionary, one of the chief meanings of the word is "to arrogate the prerogatives of God."[1] "arrogate," by the way, means "to assume, demand or challenge more than is proper; to make undue claims, from vanity or false pretensions to right or merit."[2]

When I say that the environmental movement is "blasphemous," I'm saying that the driving force behind the teaching calls God's integrity into question. I'm saying that it's a thinly veiled attempt to say that man "knows more than God does." I'm saying that the environmentalist is following after Eve in the Garden when she was told that she could be like God Himself (Gen. 3:4-5). Don't misunderstand my point. Don't get the idea that caring for God's creation is sinful in itself. The Bible makes clear that we are to act as good stewards of all that He has made, and Prov. 12:10 explicitly says that a righteous man is concerned with the welfare of his animals.

The problem develops when people get overly zealous and they begin to hold a member of the animal kingdom in higher esteem than they have for their fellow man. (I should make a parenthetical but significant insertion here, that being that man is not a member of the animal kingdom. Man is unique in all of God's creation; I expect that you will see this with ever-increasing clarity as you progress through this section of the book.) Just as we humans are "worth more than many sparrows," Jesus' sacrificial death was sufficient to put a permanent end to the slaughtering of myriads upon myriads of animals – a practice that spanned fifteen centuries – at God's direction. I can just hear the champions for the cause of protecting the northern hairy-nose wombat writhing in agony over the claim that anyone would dare to utter the words that man is more important to God than these endangered critters are. (And yes, just like the peacock spider, the northern hairy-nosed wombat is for real.)

But if the Lord's once-for-all atonement on the cross of Calvary is greater – greater by an infinite measure – than million of rams, goats, lambs, bulls, and turtledoves, we should take it as a sign that God really does value man more than He does any other creature. A lot more. Never forget that God became a *man* in order that He might die for sinful *men*. I said it once, I'll say it twice: to lower man to the level of an animal is blasphemy. However, that is the very doctrine the environmental proponent holds most dear.

9

SHE WOULDN'T HURT A WASP

I once heard a wise man say that ideas have consequences. To put a little different spin on that statement, our thoughts determine our actions. This observation reminds me of a neighbor Debbie and I had some years ago. Hanging directly over their garage door, just under the eaves, was the largest wasp's nest I'd ever seen. I happened to notice it while I was outside, talking to another neighbor. I pointed to the nest and asked my friend if he knew anything about it. He said, "Yeah, the lady who lives there is one of those tree-huggers. She says that those wasps have just as much right to her home as she does, so she won't kill them or tear the nest down."

My friend went on to say that several of the surrounding neighbors have approached the woman and asked her to do something about the pests, because they were starting to get really populous and they were becoming a threat to the homes around hers. Every time she was asked about the problem, though, the woman politely explained that "wasps are people, too," and that they needed a home just as much as any of the rest of us. I immediately picked up on the lady's hypocrisy. She lived in a house that was made of wood and stone. She surely sat on furniture that was likewise cut from trees. Her yard was lush and neatly trimmed, which means she was not against mowing and fertilizing. She had at least one car, although she parked it in the street (my friend said that she never entered or exited her house through the garage for fear that she might disturb her precious guests). I'm even willing to bet that the lady probably ran a furnace in the winter and an air conditioner in the summer.

Evidently, this dear woman failed to think things through. The simple act of mowing puts every last bug, rodent and reptile in her yard at risk, does it not? (Lawn mower blades are sharp, and they spin fast too!) Most lawn care products and fertilizers contain ingredients that are harmful to certain wildlife, and many manufacturers of these goods are actually proud of this fact! It's as though they *want* to hurt these vermin!

As dangerous as it is for those helpless little creatures to try and make a home in her grass, how much worse is it for those who want to stay inside her home? That lady doesn't know it, but she's probably running a highly successful slaughterhouse. Literally millions of dust mites and other microscopic animals are senselessly murdered every time their host decides to turn on the air conditioner or furnace, run the vacuum, or do the laundry. And then there's that awful car she drives. Imagine all the greenhouse gases her automobile is emitting, and we all know what that is doing to our fragile planet! (And her gas-powered mower and weedeater are making things even worse!)

Please forgive my sarcasm, but I'm using this literary device to drive home an important point. Imagine living next door to someone who never mows or fertilizes their yard, never vacuums, never sweeps, never shakes their rugs, never dusts, never mops their floors. They never do any laundry, and they never use climate control. Would that property not itself become a nuisance and a hazard to the whole neighborhood? Try and envision the disease and pestilence that would be rampant in that house. There would be no way you could avoid being put at risk for all manner of evil, if someone like that was your neighbor.

Fortunately for our neighborhood, the only thing this woman obsessed over, so far as anyone knew, was her pet wasps. The question that no one has dared put to her, though, is "What about the other things you're killing, just by living your life?" If that little oversight were ever brought to her attention, who knows how she might react in order to put a stop to all of her senseless butchery? As a side note, picture a world without cars, lawn equipment, home appliances, or central heat and air. Then we would have a truly "animal-friendly" place to live. But then again, we would be living in the exact same squalor that third-world countries do. I'm not ready to make that kind of commitment, and more important, nowhere in Scripture does God ask us to do so.

10

GEORGIA (GUIDESTONES) ON MY MIND

In Luke 10:10-14, Jesus said that "...whatever city you enter, and they do not receive you, go out into its streets and say, 'The very dust of your city which clings to us we wipe off against you. Nevertheless know this, that the kingdom of God has come near you.' But I say to you that it will be more tolerable in that Day for Sodom than for that city. Woe to you, Chorazin! Woe to you, Bethsaida! For if the mighty works which were done in you had been done in Tyre and Sidon, they would have repented long ago, sitting in sackcloth and ashes. But it will be more tolerable for Tyre and Sidon at the judgment than for you."

There are two kinds of unsaved people: there are those who've never heard the gospel, and there are those who've heard but rejected it. Jesus warns those who refuse Him that they will be punished more severely in eternity than those who went through life having never heard. While it's clear that Jesus is speaking of matters surrounding final judgment, our passage in Romans 1 deals with God's judgment upon a people group before the time of the end.

Lamech and his descendants were judged at the time of the Flood. As I mentioned way back yonder, Lamech left no mark on the world, since the lamp of his posterity was suddenly and permanently snuffed out in the days of Noah. It is here that I need to draw another line connecting Lamech to America. We have seen that Lamech knew *about* God, but he never came to *know* God. Our NT passage describes the same scenario. Romans 1:21 says that this judgment is reserved for people who know who God is. In vs. 24, 26, and 28, there is the repeating phrase that "God gave them up." God can't turn His back on someone unless He had at some previous point been facing in their direction.

The thought here is that God doesn't "give up" a society that never honored Him in the first place. For them, there would be nothing for God to give up. For America, though, we're like Chorazin and Bethsaida. We've been privileged to hear and know about the Savior, but recently we have begun to move away from Him. God is now following after us in judgment; He has given us up. Prepare yourself, as you read these next few paragraphs, for an explanation of the dominating premise of this book. It is my intention to show what is meant by God "giving up" on people. In later chapters, we will look at the implications of this phenomenon as vs. 26-32 describe them. Our focus in this section, however, will be trained on vs. 18-25.

This first pronouncement of God having given up, in v. 24, is a portrait in sketch form of an "unclean" community. The statement is accompanied by vivid phrases like "lusts of their hearts" and "dishonor their bodies." When people rebel against the Lord, they replace His commands with their own evil desires, which inevitably lead them into a pattern of self-destruction.

Have you ever heard of the Georgia Guidestones? Sometimes called the "American Stonehenge," this bizarre monument was erected in 1980 about 90 miles east of Atlanta. It is made of six curiously arranged granite slabs and stands about 19 feet tall. The slabs have an inscription written in eight modern languages; a short message is also at the top of the structure that is in four ancient dialects. The longer engraving, which is in the eight languages, is a set of ten guidelines. Here they are:

1. Maintain humanity under 500,000,000 in perpetual balance with nature.

2. Guide reproduction wisely – improving fitness and diversity.

3. Unite humanity with a living new language.

4. Rule passion – faith – tradition – and all things with tempered reason.

5. Protect people and nations with fair laws and just courts.

6. Let all nations rule internally resolving external disputes in a world court.

7. Avoid petty laws and useless officials.

8. Balance personal rights with social duties.

9. Prize truth – beauty – love – seeking harmony with the infinite.

10. Be not a cancer on the earth – Leave room for nature – Leave room for nature.[1]

Many volumes would have to be written in order expound all the problems this worldview espouses. Suffice it to say that every one of these ten principles is found in premillennial eschatology. The authors of this manifesto are not precisely known, but virtually everything about this shrine and its markings is coming out of what I would call "The Antichrist's Playbook." The world's final dictator, who is described in chilling detail in II Thessalonians 2 and Revelation 13, will seek to employ these very ideals in his attempt to control and eventually annihilate humanity.

This is but one example of what happens when sinful men seek to overthrow holy God. They know God, but they refuse to glorify Him as God, nor are they thankful. Their thoughts become useless, they claim to be wise but become fools, and they transfer their worship from the omnipotent Creator to a weak and dying creature. That's the starting line for the descent into hell, so says Rom. 1:21-23. And to think, the death spiral has only just begun.

11

IF YOU CAN'T BEAT THEM, SHUT 'EM UP

I want to return to the subject of climate change for a moment. Rom. 1:25 says that a nation under God's judgment will trade God's truth for "the lie." When I think of "the" lie, I think of the very first lie; it was told by Satan to Eve in the Garden of Eden. Just before she ate of the forbidden fruit, the serpent persuaded Eve with the promise that she could be like God (Gen. 3:1-6). It's the very same lie, packaged in thousands upon millions of diverse ways, which the devil is still using to deceive man. Every offense has its roots in this original sin, the sin of pride. It's the sin that man commits when he thinks he can be like God. It's the sin that soaks through every word of a freakish graven image on a hill in rural Georgia.

When man gets to this point – when he trades the truth for the lie – he won't be satisfied to just ignore the truth. He'll actively work to suppress it (Rom. 1:18). He will go out of his way to try and completely eradicate it. It's the very thing we are seeing in this furor over climate change. By the time this book reaches your hands, you may or may not be able to view a six-minute YouTube video of an exchange between Alabama senator Jeff Sessions and EPA administrator Gina McCarthy. If you can watch this brief but entertaining little dust-up, please do. Here's the address: http://www.youtube.com/watch?v=24DPluG-MEM&feature=youtube_gdata_player.

The upshot of the banter between these two people is over whether or not there is enough reliable data to prove the case for global warming. McCarthy was asking on behalf of the EPA for a 6% increase in funding for the agency. Sessions, who played devil's advocate, asked her several pointed questions about whether or not the global climate was changing, and if so, what the root cause of it was. Sen. Sessions also asked Miss McCarthy if there had been a measurable increase in hurricanes or other weather-related disasters that could be traced back to manmade "climate change." McCarthy vigorously defended her position, but she was unable to produce any evidence to defend her case.

I am going to jump into the fray for a moment and give you my two cents. As I write this page, it is March 30, 2015. I don't know when this book will be completed and published, but by the time you're reading this I'm guessing that a year or more will have elapsed. I have absolute proof that "climate change" as described and promoted by environmental activists is a hoax and a lie. What is my proof? YOU are alive and reading this!

If in fact you find yourself reading this book and the world around you has spun out of control, it will be for reasons other than how many greenhouse gases we've been belching into the atmosphere. If there's a worldwide central government that's headed up by one man, if there has been an unprecedented sudden disappearance of millions of people all over the globe, and if there's been a treaty made with the nation of Israel that's supposed to last seven years, I recommend you get your hands on my first book, "'Till He Comes: A Look at the Return of Jesus and the End of the World" (available on Amazon).

As far as evidence in my case against Mr. Gore and his disciples, these activists are providing their own proof. One such witness is Richard Parncutt, a professor at the University of Graz in Austria, who gave a written opinion about what he thought should be done with people who deny "GW" (global warming). Here is an excerpt of what he put on the university's website: "I don't think that mass murderers of the usual kind...should face the death penalty... Nor do I think tobacco denialists (sic) are guilty enough to warrant the death penalty, in spite of the enormous number of deaths that resulted more or less directly from tobacco denialism (sic). GW is different. With high probability it will cause hundreds of millions of deaths. For this reason I propose that the death penalty is appropriate for influential GW deniers. More generally, I propose that we limit the death penalty to people whose actions will with a high probability cause millions of future deaths."[1]

Mr. Parncutt's thirst for blood is beyond what many environmentalists would advocate, but he is not alone when it comes to the far-out belief that "something must be done" about people who would dare to challenge the so-called facts surrounding climate change. Read the aforementioned article for yourself. It talks about men like Gore and Robert F. Kennedy, Jr., men who want to fine or imprison people who speak out against their doctrines. Question: If climate change is true, if its claims are proven, why is there a need to persecute the dissenters? If I'm a crackpot for doubting such irrefutable science, why must I be threatened so? To borrow a line from Queen Gertrude, "The lady doth protest too much, methinks."

12

WHAT IS TRUTH?

I need to use great care in my wording here. I cannot allow man's fallible and often silly attempts to explain the mechanics of the universe to be the prevailing focus of my work. I don't know everything, and that's a fact. But my inability to fully understand a matter does not in any way impact its veracity. I don't understand what goes on inside an atomic bomb that makes it so utterly devastating, but if you were to set one off in my living room, my ignorance as to its inner workings would be of no help in lessening the destruction it would cause.

We live in an era that is frequently called "postmodern." From the time of Adam until the 17th century A.D., man lived under the philosophical paradigm of "premodernism." This is a bit of an oversimplification, but in general terms premodernism taught that truth is knowable, that it is of supreme importance, and that all truth comes from God. Then, long about the year 1650, the world experienced "Enlightenment," what many historians now call "The Age of Reason." Thomas Paine, an influential political supplicant from the late 1700's, wrote a book entitled "The Age of Reason," which was published in 1794. This work capsulized the significant elements of the Enlightenment, which asserted that while truth is both knowable and important, it can be found in a source apart from God. This era came to later be known as modernism.

Modernism was followed by postmodernism, which started creeping into Western thought in the late 19th and early 20th centuries, boldly claims that there is no "truth," but even if there is such a thing it can't be known. Furthermore, postmodernism says that if truth did exist and if it could be found, it wouldn't matter because it is unimportant. However, a terrifying new slant on postmodernism has now wormed its way into the American mindset over the last 25 years or so. Instead of denying truth, this offshoot of classical postmodern philosophy postulates that truth really is obtainable, it is knowable, and it's important. It comes, however, with a dangerous twist. This new strain argues that truth is not discovered; rather, it is determined. Many Americans today have fallen victim to the devil's scheme, the same tired old deception that man can be like God. This insidious teaching says that the individual decides for himself what is true, whereas our Lord steadfastly stands in direct opposition to this lie.

Barack Obama did a masterful job of showing what this deadly belief system looks like when he was interviewed by one Cathleen Falsani. During the interview, she asked Obama if he believed in the concept of sin. When he said he did, she asked him what sin is. His answer: "Being out of alignment with my values." She pressed him further, asking him what happens if he has sin in his life. Obama replied, "I think it's the same thing as the question about heaven. In the same way that if I'm true to myself and my faith then that is its own reward; when I'm not true to it, it's its own punishment."[1]

In just a few sentences, Obama gives us the whole package of this new postmodern thinking. He believes in sin, and he believes it's important to know what sin is. But unlike the premodern thinker (and, more to the point, the biblical thinker), Obama decides for himself what sin is, and then he takes the next logical step and says that he is the one who determines the consequences of his sin. Do you see how deleterious this worldview is? The Bible teaches that God defines sin, and God determines its consequences.

On the night before He was crucified, Jesus pleaded to the Father on behalf of us sinners. His prayer, which is found in John 17, included these precious words: "Sanctify them by Your truth. Your word is truth" (v. 17). Only a few hours after this great prayer, Jesus was standing before Pilate, the Roman governor who ultimately turned Him over to the people to be murdered. During Pilate's examination of Jesus, there was a brief discussion about this elusive concept called truth. Here is an excerpt from this interchange between them: "Jesus answered, 'You say rightly that I am a king. For this cause I was born, and for this cause I have come into the world, that I should bear witness to the truth. Everyone who is of the truth hears My voice.' Pilate said to Him, 'What is truth?' And when he had said this, he went out again to the Jews, and said to them, 'I find no fault in Him at all'" (John 18:37-38).

First, let me say that you know a society is in deep trouble when its judges mock the very suggestion of a thing called "truth." Which brings me to a personal moment with you, as I must ask you a leading question: What do you say that truth is? Please, stop reading for a second, put this book down, come up with your own definition of the word "truth," then come back and read on.

I have surveyed more than a few people on this subject of truth, and I have received back very little in the way of a majority opinion as to how to define this word. The most common response I get from Christian theologians is this frustrating answer: "All truth is God's truth." Uh, okay. What does *that* mean? The problem with this definition is that it's a statement of circular logic. It's not that the words spoken aren't true; it's just that this is only an observation. It doesn't define the word; ergo it doesn't answer the question.

The 1828 Webster Dictionary gives over a dozen meanings to the word "truth." Here is definition #1: "Conformity to fact or reality; exact accordance with that which is, or has been, shall be." It then uses the word in a couple of sample sentences: "The truth of history constitutes its whole value. We rely on the truth of the scriptural prophecies."[2]

My wife Debbie gives this as her definition of the word "truth": "Whatever God says it is." I say that it doesn't get any better than that. Just so you know, Debbie's definition is not the same as saying that "All truth is God's truth." Debbie is giving a real definition of the word, and she's assigning ownership to the reality contained in that word. Hers is a simple but perfectly concise conclusion that what God says is what truth is. I know of nothing more important than to understand this marvelous thing.

I had planned to close this section of the book with grand expositions on social ills of the religious and political left, stuff like Agenda 21 and Sustainable Development, like Obamacare and Race to the Top. But do you know what? I'm not going to get sucked into that trap. As I progress through this work, I'll give you plenty of examples of the world's misbegotten and dissipating values, just to give you a sense for where we are and how far down the shaft of God's judgment that we have fallen. I am not, however, going to dump layer upon layer of every little goofball thought that man has conjured up to try and prove my case. This way, I'm freeing myself up to write more about what God says, which is infinitely greater and more important than all the collective statements of our sin-ravaged race throughout all of history put together.

I don't know everything. You don't know everything. Man has a tendency to disbelieve the things he can't explain or doesn't understand. That's where faith comes in. As you continue to read, my prayer for you is that you will seek wisdom and exercise discernment, that you will disregard all error and hold fast to the truth. It is, after all, whatever God says it is.

PART TWO

VILE PASSIONS

"For this reason God gave them up to vile passions. For even their women exchanged the natural use for what is against nature. Likewise also the men, leaving the natural use of the woman, burned in their lust for one another, men with men committing what is shameful, and receiving in themselves the penalty of their error which was due" – Romans 1:26-27

13

TWO WIVES, ONE HOME

The timeline from our nation's founding down to the present hour is dotted with numerous milestones, events that caused sudden and drastic shifts in the course the country would travel. In recent decades, we might point to the notorious Roe v. Wade decision of 1973, which legalized the killing of the most defenseless people on earth. Many Christians believe that this was when God began to turn His back on America.

Others may place their fingers a decade or so earlier on the continuum, when the Supreme Court ruled that prayer in the public schools was unconstitutional.[1] Still others may push the date that God left America even further back, to 1947, when the nation's highest court made an aberrant ruling in the case that inserted the anti-constitutional language "separation of Church and State" into constitutional case law.[2]

I am inclined to look at a time even more distant. The years that followed the close of the Industrial Revolution in the late 1800's were marred by the introduction of liberalism into the American church. The last half of the 19th century saw numerous ingredients – many of them undetected but all of them poisonous – tunnel their way into the minds and pulpits of countless influential theologians. In particular, the onset of materialistic greed created by the burgeoning middle class and a misbegotten religion made popular by the likes of Darwin and Lyell combined to make a piquant, inviting, zesty, and destructive meal that was hungrily devoured by the masses.

Whether we're talking about abortion, public prayer, or the daughters of evolution (which brought the world the horrors of everything from the Holocaust to Planned Parenthood), they all hold in common the same error found in the preposterous "separation of Church and State" edict. It's the same blunder that Lamech made. He incorrectly deduced that he could compartmentalize his life into the secular and the sacred. If he were alive today, Lamech would have been a faithful churchgoer and maybe even a leader in his congregation. However, he would have lived quite comfortably in his sin most of the week and then he'd show up Sunday morning ready to give his testimony about how good God is to him because they're such great pals.

Lamech boasted thusly to his two wives, one of whom he should never have had. The fallout from that, of course, is that he and his posterity became virtual unknowns to the chroniclers of history. More important, Lamech is now and ever shall be paying for his sin the place of everlasting perdition.

America has now been poured into Lamech's cast. We brag about our greatness to our two wives, Church and State. We've married two women, having forgotten that God had arranged for the two to become one (Gen. 2:24). Lamech was unsuccessful when he tried to squeeze an extra person into the two-into-one equation. We're failing in like manner, and unless we learn from our sin and repent of it, we'll keep on growing weaker and weaker until we're just another moldy crust at the bottom of history's garbage can.

14

IN THE CHURCH AS IT IS AT HOME

You've probably heard the same arguments that I have when it comes to God being some kind of misogynist. Here are a few passages from the epistles that have stuck in the craw of many a liberated American woman over the past 50 years or so: I Cor. 11:3, 7-9; Eph. 5:22-24; Col. 3:18; Tit. 2:3-5; I Pet. 3:1-6.

You may very well be able to recite many of these verses from memory, but I want to ask you to please take a few moments and read them all in rapid succession. Just as I wrote the words above – "rapid succession" – I put my pen down and read those verses, too. If I were to summarize them and condense them into one sentence, I'd word it something like this: "But I want you to know that the head of every man is Christ, the head of woman is man, and the head of Christ is God" (I Cor. 11:3).

One of the most dangerous methods of Bible study is to cherry-pick from the Scriptures. Take a verse from the Pentateuch, a verse or two out of one of the gospels, another couple of verses from over there in the minor prophets, put them in a blender, turn it on high, and the next thing you know you've made for yourself a nice little messed-up and petty doctrine. I need to interject that the verses above aren't an example of this, because all of them are addressing the same theme: leadership and submission.

However, it's easy to zero in on the part about submission and ignore the other side of this coin. Let's fill in a few gaps here so as to avoid puncturing holes in sound doctrine. This time, go back and read "the rest of the story." Read I Cor. 11:11-12; Eph. 5:25-33; Col. 3:19; Tit. 2:1-2, 6-8; I Pet. 3:7. Just as I did with the other verses, I'd like to summarize these. Ready? "But I want you to know that the head of every man is Christ, the head of woman is man, and the head of Christ is God" (I Cor. 11:3).

This one verse doesn't give a lot of details, but it is a wonderful summary of God's diagram for society. Keep your finger in I Corinthians 11, and flip a couple of pages to the right and find Chapter 14. When you get there, read v. 33. I see this verse as a companion to 11:3 because it, too, is a summary statement. God is not a God of confusion. The Greek word "akatastasia" means "instability, disorder; commotion, confusion, tumult." Instead, God is "eirene," which is Greek for "peace; by implication, prosperity: one, peace, quietness, rest, set at one again." Even a casual reading of I Corinthians reveals that the church in Corinth was a madhouse, and God did not like it that way.

At no point in Scripture does God ever condone His people acting in a disorderly fashion, whether they're in corporate worship or sitting in their living room. Look at the verse above, v. 32, which is another compendious remark about how God's people should behave. Notice that the "prophets" (those who are leading the worship services) are to be in total control at all times, as their spirit is constantly in subjection to their mind.

Take this spiritual truth with you now back to Chapter 11 and v. 3. There are four persons listed here: man, Christ, woman, and God. God (the Father) is the head of Christ (God the Son). Christ is the head of the man, and the man is the head of the woman. God does all things in an orderly fashion, so it makes perfect sense that He has established a hierarchy that He expects to be modeled by His children.

Before we launch into a discussion on how this ranking system should look, you need to know that God's plan here does not in any way reflect the value of a person's worth. People love to jump to the conclusion that if a woman is to be in submission to her husband, then she is somehow less important than her mate. If that is the case, then Jesus is inferior to God the Father, and we know that is absolutely <u>not</u> true! (See John 10:30; Phil. 2:6; Col. 1:15, 19; I Tim. 3:16; Heb. 1:1-3.) Jesus is not beneath the Father in any way, shape, or form. He does, however, voluntarily place Himself in a subordinate position, which is why He always does the will of the Father (John 5:30; 6:38; 8:29).

Jesus set the pattern for us to follow in all things (John 13:15; Rom. 8:29; I Cor. 11:1; Eph. 5:1-2; Phil. 2:5; I Pet.

2:21; I John 2:5-6; 3:16), which means that we are in subjection to Him just as he has placed Himself under the headship of the Father. In addition, it means that women are of no less worth than men any more than the Son is to the Father. We already saw this in I Pet. 3:7, where men are told to give honor to their wives because men and women alike are heirs together of all the gifts that come with salvation.

Now that we've got that point settled, keep your eyes trained on I Cor. 11:3 for just a little longer. The Father is the "head" of Christ, Christ is the "head" of the man, and the man is the "head" of the woman. The Greek word for "head" in this verse speaks of a person who is in the role of supremacy or lordship. The Son always does the will of the father, so it stands to reason that the man is to seek the will of Christ and the woman is to follow her husband willingly. This is how the Christian home is to be run.

With this model of the home in mind, turn back now to I Corinthians 14. We saw in v. 33 that God is not present in chaos and anarchy, and Paul makes it obvious here that he is speaking specifically to the church when it meets for worship. This time, though, keep reading. Go ahead and read v. 33 again, but add to it vs. 34-35. Do you see how beautifully this all fits together? The leadership of the church is supposed to mirror the leadership of the home!

I can almost sense the discomfort that some of you may be having about this, so I'm going to play hot potato for a moment and let you hear from another source. Writing a brief elucidation on vs. 34-40, David Jeremiah offers some excellent insights. He writes: "With their newfound freedom in Christ, many women in the Corinthian church were speaking up and speaking out in worship service, adding to the confusion being caused by the chaotic use of gifts within that assembly. For the sake of peace and unity, the women were instructed to voice their thoughts at home. Knowing this might be controversial, Paul challenges those who think that they are spiritual to check him on these points (I Thess. 2:13; II Tim. 3:15-17; II Pet. 1:19-21). Everything the church does, he concludes, should 'be done decently and in order,' especially worship services."[1]

The bottom line is that the polity of the church and the single-family home are identical. Christ is the head of the body (i.e. the church, cf. Eph. 5:23-24; Col. 1:18) as well as the home. Since God runs His institutions in an orderly, predictable, consistent pattern, it would be completely against His nature to have the man lead the home and then give the leadership of the church to the woman. If He did that, what message would it send to the youngsters in the church or to the outside observers?

God does unpredictable things all the time, but the methods He employs in performing the everyday tasks are always uniform in nature. When Lamech turned his two-become-one home into a love triangle, he shoved God and

His ways out the front door. When Christians try to live a schizophrenic life by laboring to please themselves at home or work and then please God on Sunday, they have no reasonable expectation that God will give them His blessing. As Lamech probably learned (only too late), God is either first in your life or He's dead last. There is no middle ground.

15

LADIES FIRST

Romans 1:26 says that when society spurns God, He turns them over to "vile passions." I find it fascinating that the verse concludes with the decree that the nation's women, not the men, are the ones who take the lead in the sexual revolt. Once the female population has set the wheels of insurrection in motion, the men fall in line behind them (v. 27). How many times in history have we seen it play out like this? Eve led Adam into sin (Gen. 3:6; I Tim. 2:12-14). Sarai lost her trust in the Lord, and she gave Abram the idea to commit adultery (Gen. 16:1-4). Even Solomon, the wisest man who ever lived, couldn't resist falling into a trap that was set by his many wives (I Kings 11:1-10).

And how about Ahab? Borrowing again from David Jeremiah, he writes this about Jezebel in I Kings 16:30-31: "When Ahab married Jezebel, he violated every principle God had ever given him. Jezebel was a pagan, and she brought all of her wicked religion with her into Israel. She persuaded Ahab to build a temple and altar to Baal in Samaria, where Ahab was. She supported 850 prophets of her immoral cult, and she systematically went through Israel, trying to kill all the prophets of Yahweh that she could find. King Jehu referred to her ways as 'harlotries' and 'witchcraft' (II Kings 9:22). Ahab did not have the spiritual courage or conviction to stop Jezebel, and so he followed her example and committed great evil (21:25)."[1]

Speaking of Jezebel, there was a woman who led the church astray, and it drew the attention of our Lord Jesus. He was incensed by the assembly at Thyatira because they were putting up with the wicked antics of a female leader in their midst (Rev. 2:18-23). So you see, whether we're talking about the home, the king's palace, the church, or society at large, women possess tremendous power. God knows that when men abandon the leadership role that He expressly gave to them, the danger arises that women will step in and take charge. This is a scenario that God never intended to happen, so who knows what trouble may befall the home or church or nation that dares to test Him in this?

I know we've used several other guinea pigs in this chapter, but I haven't forgotten about Lamech. Neither Adah nor Zillah, his two wives, are mentioned in Scripture outside of Gen. 4:19-24. Furthermore, the Bible records not so much as a single word spoken by either woman. These facts make it tough to lay any blame on the women of Lamech's home, which is exactly the point. The problem in Lamech's life wasn't his wives; the problem in Lamech's life was Lamech. It is good that Lamech appeared to be the head of his house, but that's all the good that we can derive from him.

Look at how he spoke to them. In Gen. 4:23, he begins to lecture these women, and he starts with these words: "Adah and Zillah, hear my voice; Wives of Lamech, listen to my speech!" If I started a discussion with my wife using that kind of talk, I'd probably get a frying pan bashed upside my head! And you know what? That's what *should* happen! Lamech showed his wives no tenderness whatsoever. He had the "I'm the ruler of my castle, king over all I survey" part down pat. What he didn't have was love and respect for his family. As we already saw in multiple scriptures just a few pages back, husbands are to love their wives and give them honor.

Here's a question for Lamech: "You married Adah first. After you married her, how did you approach her about the subject of taking Zillah into your home?" Second question: "How did you go about telling Zillah that she was coming into a place where she'd have to share you with a woman who was there ahead of you?" As I demonstrated in the previous chapter, leadership and dictatorship are two different things. Adrian Rogers used to say to the men in his church that "Just because God has made you the head of the house, that doesn't mean that you get to be 'Little Lord Ha-Ha' and order your wife around like she's your own personal slave."

The good husband is a good leader, which means he is a servant to his wife (Eph. 5:25-29). The wise husband is the man who marries a wise woman and who will seek her counsel. In Ex. 4:24-26, Moses' wife Zipporah stepped in and did his job for him, the work of circumcising their son. Her quick action saved Moses' very own life! Moses married a wise woman, and she was therefore of great value to him.

I Samuel 25 tells the story of another wise woman; her name was Abigail. Unlike Zipporah, Abigail got stuck with one of the most foolish men in the Bible. Nabal was his name, and he was so foolish that even his very name meant "fool" (I Sam. 25:25)! Nabal was the polar opposite of Moses. Both Zipporah and Abigail did their best to protect their husbands from danger when they were misbehaving, but only Moses responded intelligently to his wife's attempts to assist him. Abigail went way above and beyond the call of duty to be her husband's helper, but Nabal was such a hardheaded imbecile he shunned her support and he died in his sin.

When a man is a fool, he rejects those who try to help him, and he will die in his sin. When a man is a tyrant (like Lamech), he will abuse and destroy his family, and he will die in his sin. When he is spineless and weak, like Ahab was, his wife will take over, and he will die in his sin. Only when a man is an upright and humble leader who is able to heed sound advice (like Moses did) will he repent of his sin, learn from it, and live.

The sexual revolution of the 1960s started with women. Betty Friedan's 1963 book "The Feminine Mystique" quickly became the feminist movement's bible. In 1966, Friedan cofounded and was elected first president of the National Organization for Women (NOW), a structured lobby for feminist causes that has since branched out into other arenas, such as fighting for abortion rights and advancing the homosexual agenda. Friedan, along with journalist Gloria Steinem and activist/actress Jane Fonda, became the standard-bearers for the campaign to destroy God's plan for the family.

The war against the married, monogamous home was in full swing by the late 60s, but the men never even donned their battle fatigues. Here we are, nearly fifty years later, and the men are still on the sidelines. Women started this conflict, but the men were too busy being a Lamech, an Ahab, or a Nabal to stop it. In fact, had they been more like Moses, maybe the battle lines would never have been drawn. But since the women took the lead and put the train on the track, the men have done what Scripture says they'd do: they followed after them.

16

LIKEWISE ALSO THE MEN

The first step of disobedience to God is the rejection of what He has revealed to man. The evidence for God is so overwhelming that man can't just ignore God; he must *suppress* (another way of saying he "actively fights against") the truth of God. This is the second step. Just an observation, but have you ever noticed that atheists can't keep silent about the subject of God? It's been my experience that atheists talk more about God than most Christians do. I once heard a Christian apologist say that there are two tenets to the atheist religion: (1) There is no God; and (2) I hate Him.

Step One is the rejection of God's revelation of Himself. Step Two is the suppression of that revelation. Now for Step Three. Because man was created with the innate desire to worship, he redirects his affections away from his Creator and toward what the Creator has made. This kind of worship can manifest itself in the worship of animals, other humans, the self, or any combination of the three. As we have seen, Lamech worshiped at the altar of self, particularly in the area of unrestrained sexual gratification.

America has been illumined to the ways of God more than any nation in history besides Israel, the Lord's precious people of promise. I was born in 1964, and the space between my youth and the present day has been marked by the rejection, suppression, and replacement of God at greater speed and by a higher percentage of Americans than perhaps anyone could have predicted. We are now entering into the fourth phase of God's judgment: sexual perversion.

Eve ate the forbidden fruit and then handed it to Adam, who did nothing to stop her from sinning and chose instead to do just as she did. King Ahab, easily one of the worst rulers Israel ever had, wimped out on virtually every occasion he had to correct his ruthless wife. A terrific example of how the royal couple lived is found in I Kings 21:1-16. It's the sad story of how wicked Jezebel plotted to murder a man named Naboth, then take his land and give it to Ahab. The king was so fainthearted that he never lifted a finger or uttered a single word to keep Jezebel from carrying out her mischievous scheme.

Thanks to too many American men abandoning their post as leaders and "watchmen" over their families, innumerable women stepped in and fulfilled duties that God never intended for them to perform. What came with these new responsibilities was a desire for more "freedom," which found its way into the realm of sexual expression. It says in Rom. 1:26 that the women traded in the "natural use" for something unnatural. The Greek word for "natural" is "physikos," and it means "physical, instinctive." The word "use" here in the NKJV is talking about "relations," specifically sexual intercourse. After the women took leave of their God-ordained sexual roles, the men fell in line behind their wives (just like Adam did, just like Ahab did). Verse 26 gives the draft that was drawn up by the women, then v. 27 shows how the men traced right over the sketch. It uses those same two words, "natural use." It's a bit crude perhaps, but a proper rendering of the first part of v. 27 would say that the men declined to have normal sexual relations with women and opted instead to fulfill their desires with one another.

Before you try to hunt me down so you can stick your finger in my face and call me names like "bigot" or "hater" (hater – what a childish term!), or use nonexistent made-up words against me like "homophobe," let me stop you right where you are. I did not say these things about homosexuality; GOD did. I am not a "homophobe." I am a "theophobe." Do you know what that is? That's a person who is afraid to call "good" something that God clearly says is bad. Verse 26 calls these perverse acts "vile passions." Verse 27 says that homosexual acts are "shameful." Again, that's not me talking; GOD said it. I must make myself clear on this point: If God said it, the whole world can deny it, and it changes nothing.

The sequence of events starts with the men, specifically when the men stop acting like men. This falls into the next domino, which is where the women get frustrated with the men and seek to reverse the roles, in a manner of speaking. Once the women get settled into a pattern of rebellion, the men will discard God's plan for sexual pleasure and they will replace the women with other men. The Bible provides us with a vivid illustration of how this last part looks. Please read Gen. 19:1-11; this was the last sinful act committed by the city of Sodom before God annihilated it.

The curtain rises (vs. 1-3) on the entrance gate to Sodom, where Lot would have been helping conduct the city's business. (Verse 9 says that he was a judge for the town, and since community leaders in those days often held meetings at their city gates, it seems likely that this is what was going on here. This in turn means that Lot was a respected leader in the community.) If there was in fact a city council meeting going on at the time, it's significant to note that Lot was the only one to welcome two strangers who had just arrived on Sodom's doorstep.

I don't know if there were other townspeople present when the strangers showed up, but we can know for certain that they were aware of this visitation because of the continuing narrative. Read vs. 4-5, and you'll see that <u>all</u> the men of Sodom, both young and old, showed up at Lot's house and surrounded it. These men knew that their town had been invaded by two men, they knew that Lot was showing them the kind of hospitality that was customarily extended to alien travelers, and they knew that they wanted to engage in acts of perversion with their angelic guests.

Go on and read vs. 6-8. Lot left the safety of his home, went outside, and tried to reason with these lustful men. He foolishly attempted to satisfy their cravings by offering them his own daughters. As repulsive as his suggestion was, Lot understood that what these men wanted was even worse! This is where the judgment of God really kicks in. Read now v. 9, and we see that the men actually and completely abandoned the "natural use" of the woman and chose instead to gratify their urges with other men, just like Romans 1 describes.

Lot, his home, and all who occupied it were now in grave danger. Finish this section of Scripture and read vs. 10-11. The angels step in at this point and save the day. They pulled Lot back into the house, and then they struck all of their would-be assailants with blindness. I don't know about anyone else, but if I were among a group of people and every one of us got struck blind all at once, my first inclination would be to go on home. But not these men. They literally wore themselves out trying to find the door so they could accomplish what they had gone there to do.

I remember hearing John MacArthur once say of this passage that the unsaved man will enter into hell "sweating." He explained that the pull of sin is very great, and the unregenerate man will work himself to death in a desperate attempt to satisfy all that his sinful mind and body yearns for.

II Peter 2:6 gives the Cliffs' Notes of the sad end to Sodom, which is given in thorough detail in Gen. 19:12-29. The next verse (II Pet. 2:7) calls Lot "righteous," and v. 8 goes on to explain why: Lot was in torment over the impish behavior of his neighbors. God had justified Lot, and Lot is now in heaven. That's really great, but I can't help but believe Lot's reward would have been much greater had he done more to warn the citizens of Sodom of their need for repentance.

Isn't that one of the primary responsibilities of the Christian, to warn people of coming judgment? That's what Noah did. That's what Moses did. It's what Isaiah and Jeremiah and Ezekiel did. Amos, Jonah, Malachi – that's what they all did. In the NT, it's what every single apostle did. And John the Baptist, Stephen, James, and Jude… same thing. And oh, yeah, Jesus did it. (For further reading on the warnings that our Lord gave His hearers, check out Matt. 7:13-23; 11:20-24; 18:6-7; chapters 23-25; and the book of Revelation.)

America is chock-full of Lamechs. There are plenty of people who call on the name of the Lord, but they have no idea who He is. We also have more than our fair share of Lots. They know the Lord, they're blood-bought believers, but they keep their faith to themselves. They cower in the corners, wringing their hands over the latest volley sent over the wall by their godless leaders, and they respond with absolutely nothing. What the world needs now, more than ever, is for godly <u>men</u> to step out of the shadows and to start acting like the salt and light that God has said we are.

17

THE NEW NORMAL

I have already drawn your attention to the bellicose nature of the dogged atheist. I don't know anyone who talks more about God than those who've made it their mission in life to disprove His existence. (On a personal level, I'd like to add that I sometimes wonder if anyone out there is determined to dispute the existence of Allah or the pantheon of Hindu gods or the deities worshiped by Wiccans.) Anyway, just as the militant unbeliever burns lots of hours and calories trying to get others to hate God as much as they do, the same can be said of those who are devoted to the cause of sexual contumacy.

The homosexual lobby has become steadily more demanding since the turn of the 21st century. Simple logic allows us to conclude that if the homosexual lifestyle were normal and healthy, there would be no reason for the proponents of it to try and foist their sin upon the heterosexual world.

The homosexual activists are every bit as relentless and insistent as are the God-haters, which can only mean one thing: they know that what they're doing is wrong. Consider the lengths to which they've gone in order to try and normalize their behavior. Take, for example, the fact that homosexuals have developed their own slang and terminology. The most basic word used to identify a homosexual is the word "gay." This word's definition was originally as follows: "merry; airy; jovial; sportive; frolicksome; fine; showy."[1] Since the mid-1800s, when this was what the word meant, it has slowly morphed into the meaning it holds today.

As you might guess, there are a myriad of terms that the homosexual counterculture has borrowed and then redefined. I am aware of what some of this jargon means, but reasonable prudence dictates that I not disclose or discuss the matter much further. What I want to make clear here is the fact that when people come together in a common cause, it's only natural that they develop their own dialect. People in the church often use "churchy" sounding words that the rest of the world seldom use and, at best, only vaguely understand. This is true of virtually every vocation and profession as well.

The same can be said of those involved in the use of illicit drugs or the gambling industry. People who live as homosexuals are no different. The homosexual movement has its own vernacular, to be sure, but it has also tapped ordinary things and converted them into their own icons. Wikipedia says this about the homosexuals' adoption of the rainbow, which is usually represented in the form of a flag: "The rainbow flag, commonly the gay pride flag and sometimes the LGBT pride flag, is a symbol of lesbian, gay, bisexual, and transgender (LGBT) pride and LGBT movements... The colors reflect the diversity of the LGBT community, and the flag is often used as a symbol of gay pride in LGBT rights marches. It originated in California, but is now used worldwide."[2]

Other tokens, such as pink triangles that were used to identify homosexuals in the Nazi concentration camps, have been resurrected. Sympathizers of the homosexual counterculture wear them today in a show of support for the movement. But I want to stay on the rainbow subject for just a moment longer, because the origin of the rainbow's meaning should be important to all Christians. Read Gen. 9:8-17, and you will discover that the rainbow was given by God as a sign to all creation that He would never destroy the earth by water again. After the Flood, God told Noah that the rainbow was a visible reminder that this would be a one-time event, never to be repeated. (Also see Psalm 104:6-9.)

I don't know which is worse, people who are trapped in their sin who steal a universally recognized sign from God to all mankind, or the failure of Christians to offer any resistance to it. We have no record that either of Lamech's wives ever spoke up when he drew the baseless and unwarranted conclusion that God would protect him from the reasonably expected consequences of his sin. Today, the American church has been equally voiceless over the blasphemous misuse of God's preferred symbols that He uses for the express purpose of communicating with His creation.

I do not speak of the rainbow here by coincidence. A grand total of eight people entered the ark (Gen. 7:7; cf. I Pet. 3:18-20), and not of them was a descendant of Lamech. I wonder what would have become of the name of Lamech had just one of his wives spoken up and inserted a little bit of wisdom into that one-sided conversation. It's impossible for me to know how this hypothetical situation might have turned out, but this "new normal" that Lamech introduced was met with the complete annihilation of his family, not to mention a world of sinners who took after him.

I suppose a case could be made in defense of the passivity showed by Lamech's spouses. Everything I've read about the people of antiquity consistently claims that women across the board had virtually no say in anything. I have a response to this argument. We've already seen that Zipporah (Moses' wife) was no shrinking violet, and her courage was what spared her husband's life. Furthermore, we saw a couple of other women from the Old Testament, such as Abigail, who made a vital impact in the lives of others thanks to their wise and calculated actions. Over and over again, throughout Scripture and throughout history, God uses a tiny minority to carry out His plans. Have you noticed that God also routinely uses the most *unlikely* people to be His servants?

Lamech was only one man, but his immoral lifestyle was never rebuked. His sinful ways caught on, and before anyone knew it there was a boat with eight people and a select group of animals floating all alone on the surface of the waters. Everyone and everything else perished. The body of Christ is now faced with a tough decision. We have the option of taking the path of least resistance and surrendering to the demands of an angry minority, determined to redefine and restructure the most basic and most essential institution in society, i.e. the family. There's a better alternative, though, and that is to be like Zipporah and tell the world "NO!"

The waves of God's judgment continue to thrash and pound against the dam of His mercy. We are already seeing great fissures developing in that dam. No one has the right to steal away God's visible reminder of a promise He made to the world so that they can corrupt its intended meaning. The word "gay" means "happy," and the rainbow is God's signature on the parchment of the sky. They are not for sale, not at any price.

When the dam breaks, we will either be safe in the ark of God's protection, or we'll be dragged to the bottom of the ocean of God's wrath. God has commanded that we stand firm against every form of evil. We find this edict in a number of places in Scripture. Here is but a sampling: "Depart from evil and do good; Seek peace and pursue it" (Psalm 34:14). "You who love the Lord, hate evil!" (Psalm

97:10a). “I will set nothing wicked before my eyes; I hate the work of those who fall away; It shall not cling to me (Psalm 101:3). “Through your precepts I get understanding; Therefore I hate every false way” (Psalm 119:104). “The fear of the Lord is to hate evil; Pride and arrogance and the evil way And the perverse mouth I hate” (Prov. 8:13). “Let love be without hypocrisy. Abhor what is evil. Cling to what is good” (Rom. 12:9).

18

THE CABOOSE OF A LONG TRAIN

As the homosexual movement began to advance and become more organized, it crept into people's thinking by redefining their vocabulary. Then it corrupted people's beliefs by twisting their religion. Having confounded what we think and what we believe, our society is now poised to take the final step, which is converting what we think and what we believe into what we do. We no longer regard marriage as being what it has always been, so now it is something that it has never been.

Just so you know, this last step – societal approval of sin – is the terminal move in the sequence of God's judgment: "...knowing the righteous judgment of God, that those who practice such things are deserving of death, not only do the same but *also approve of those who practice them*" (Rom. 1:32, emphasis mine). I know of no society in history that survived the acceptance of any "new" definition of marriage. Once that genie is out of the bottle, there is little hope for putting him back. If the word "marriage" comes to mean anything other than one man and one woman, the institution of the family crumbles. If two men can marry, or if two women can, what will stand in the way of making marriage between three people, or ten people, or between people and creatures, or between people and inanimate objects?

You might be saying, "That will never happen." But you would be wrong; it's already happening. In 1994, two men in New York City registered as "domestic partners." When they moved to Pennsylvania, though, their union became invalid. To make their home legal, one of the men, Bill Novak, adopted his boyfriend, Norman MacArthur, as his son. Now that homosexuals can "marry" in Pennsylvania, the men had their adoption nullified (because it's not yet legal for parents to marry their offspring). Their action released them from their father-son relationship (which was never their intent, as it only served their purpose of making them a legally recognized family), so now they can be husband and husband instead of father and son.[1]

In 2012, one Nadine Schweigert of North Dakota had a ceremony to celebrate her marriage to herself.[2] In my search for that news clip (for I'd heard about it before I researched it), I came across an article about an Australian woman who married a tree, another in Seattle who married a public building, and, well, that's quite far enough. The point is that if marriage doesn't have a unique and specific definition, then marriage can be anything. If marriage can mean anything, it means *nothing*. If it means nothing, then everything constitutes a "family." If everything is a family, then *nothing* is a family.

If society has no definable family, the society ceases to exist.

To repeat, there is no nation, kingdom, or empire in all of history that ever survived its willingness to accept a contaminated version of marriage and the family. The American church, just like Lamech's wives, is wilting in the face of opposition. Lamech was outnumbered by the rest of the world. Do you know why he got away with marrying two women instead of one? Do you know why he bragged about killing a man with impunity? Do you know how he cultivated a gross misunderstanding of God and His ways? Because no one would correct him. Why is America (and now the world) in such a pickle? Because the church, the only entity on earth who knows where to find the truths of God, cringes and quakes in terror when a few misguided people pop off against God and His elect.

I don't know how many times I've heard someone say, "I don't care what anyone does, so long as it doesn't affect me." Everyone should know by now that what a person does always affects others. If your town, your state, or your country accepts sexual perversion as a viable lifestyle, does your family know where *you* stand on the matter? If you think it's okay for people you don't know to stay caught in the trap of their sin, your children and grandchildren will have to know whether or not you think it's okay for them to choose that kind of life for themselves. If you find it acceptable for your fellow man to live and die in his sin, you must be able to articulate to your friends, your spouse, and your little ones what their options are and why.

If a profligate lifestyle is permissible for the stranger, why is it taboo for the loved one? Didn't Jesus command us to love our neighbor? There is nothing happy about the life of the "gay" person. It is typically filled to overflowing with love triangles, physical and emotional abuse, promiscuity, disease, violence, drug and alcohol addiction, and drastically shortened life expectancy. It's been rightly said that homosexuality is not a "lifestyle," but rather a "deathstyle." Are you prepared to tell your family that such a sad and reprehensible way to live is suitable for anyone?

The homosexual is not just a man or a woman who engages in an act against nature every so often. The homosexual is a person whose entire life is consumed by a warped worldview. Nearly everything he thinks, says, and does is affected by his view of sex. The word "homosexual" has a meaning far beyond a description of perceived sexual preferences. It is a word that defines every aspect of who a person is. It's no wonder the Scripture says that the men "burned in their lust for one another" (Rom. 1:27). The Greek words for "burned" and "lust" are both graphic and explicit terms. They describe a person whose entire being – body, mind, and soul – is completely eaten up with uncontrollable desire. That's why the men of Sodom wore themselves out trying to satisfy their urges, even after God had struck all of them blind!

19

HOLLOW ARGUMENTS

One popular argument the world likes to use against the church is to say that the Bible does not make clear God's position on sexual perversion. I should hope that the last few chapters have successfully dispelled that myth. In addition, passages like Lev. 18:22; 20:13; I Cor. 6:9-10; I Tim. 1:9-11; Rev. 21:8 make God's views on the matter as clear as they can possibly be.

Even the homosexual lobby knows how clear the Bible is. It is so unambiguous that a pro-homosexual group saw the need to mutilate the Scriptures and come up with their own version of the Bible. Called the Queen James Bible, the editors took numerous liberties with several significant verses in both the Old and New Testaments in an attempt to cleanse God's Word of anti-homosexual content.[1] The mere publication of this document proves beyond all doubt at least two things. First, it verifies the fact that the Bible is clear to the extreme in proclaiming God's final statement of the matter. Second, it demonstrates the lengths to which sympathizers will go in order to try and legitimize this deviant behavior.

Another argument that is relentlessly made by pro-homosexual groups is that sexual preference is a genetically inherited trait. The concept being promoted here is that sexual desire for one gender over the other is the direct result of genetic predisposition. Pop star Lady Gaga set her opinion on the matter to music with the song "Born This Way." (I'll let you look up the lyrics online, if you're interested. I see no edifying or redeeming value in publishing them here.) The gist of the song is that it is a vivid apologetic for the notion that people are homosexual by birth, not by choice.

I have several responses to this reasoning. First, there are many people who have left homosexuality and become heterosexuals. Joe Dallas is one such man. He grew up as a homosexual, but he is now a married heterosexual. He has a ministry that is aimed at addressing all kinds of sexually related sins, particularly homosexuality. (You can find much more information about Mr. Dallas and his work on his websites, thesexualresolution.com and joedallas.com.)

Another high-profile former homosexual is Christian singer/songwriter Dennis Jernigan. Go to his website (dennisjernigan.com), and you can read all about his personal testimony, which includes his triumph over homosexuality.

My second response to the contention that people can't control which gender they prefer is that even homosexuals know that this argument is a façade. Sally Kohn, journalist and homosexual activist, has openly said that she is a homosexual and that she wants her daughter to grow up to be a homosexual.

In a news article where Miss Kohn expresses those very words, she also writes this: "Time will tell, but so far, it doesn't look like my 6-year-old daughter is gay. In fact, she's boy crazy. It seems early to me, but I'm trying to be supportive. Recently, she had a crush on an older boy on her school bus. She was acting as any precocious, socially awkward child would, which is to say not very subtle. I confided in a friend who has an older daughter. 'She wants to give this kid a card and presents,' I e-mailed. 'The other kid is so embarrassed. It's painful to watch. What do I do?' My friend wrote back with a slew of helpful advice, ending with a punch to my gut: 'Bet it wouldn't bother you so much if her crush was on a girl.' She was right. I'm a slightly overbearing pro-gay mom. But I'm going to support my daughter, whatever choices she makes."[2]

Query: Why is Sally Kohn concerned about her daughter's sexual proclivities? If the gender she finds herself most attracted to is part of her genetic makeup, why should Sally care? If the daughter has no control over whether she prefers boys or girls, then it's obvious that what her mother wants for her child is completely irrelevant. By her own admission, Miss Kohn is a homosexual by choice, not by birth. In this respect, homosexuality is a sin like every other sin; it is an act of the will. This means that you can choose to sin in this manner, or you can choose not to.

Going back to the "God did not make Himself clear" polemic, this ties in with the infantile allegation that people who speak out against homosexuality are guilty of "hate speech." Let there be no doubt that no man, not even a Christian, was the first to identify homosexuality as a sinful act. God declared it. What I am writing in this book cannot be properly labeled as "hate speech." What I'm writing is "love speech." For a person to downplay the severity of this sin, knowing what God says the outcome of it will be, *that* is the pinnacle of hatred.

Let me tell you a little secret about myself. I hope you're sitting down for this. I, Ted Merritt, am a sinner. You read that right; I'm not perfect. Homosexuality is definitely not a temptation for me, but I have sinned in a seemingly unlimited number of other ways throughout my whole life. I'm a Christian, and I love the Lord Jesus with all my might, but I'm not able to retire from my more than 50-year career as a professional transgressor. I am a Christian because I understand that I need to be a Christian. I have to be a Christian, for the singular alternative to it is that I end up in hell for eternity.

A vital characteristic of the Christian is that Christians do not try to diminish the gravity of their sins. Equally important is the fact that Christians should never want another person to minimize or dismiss the gravity of their sin. As a Christian, it is my responsibility to regularly examine myself in light of Scripture and to continually make determinations to see if I am truly a child of God (see II Cor. 13:5). I neither expect nor want anyone to permit me to wallow in any sin that has overtaken me (cf. Gal. 6:1). I am committed to extending that courtesy to others as well. People can call me names like "hater" if they want, but God is unmoved in how He defines sin. I am to love people enough that I should never fail to warn them when it is apparent that they have been ensnared by their sin, regardless of the cost to me. It is every Christian's job to look after his neighbor, to be a watchman for both the saved and the unsaved (see Ezekiel 33:1-6).

20

DEMANDING OUR HOLINESS

Another counterpoint to the belief that a desire for sexual irregularity can't be helped is that this is a direct attack on God's character. If God has made it plain that homosexuality is a sin (which He has done, in spades), then God promises that homosexuality, like all sins, can be avoided. In I Cor. 10:13, Paul writes: "No temptation has overtaken you except such as is common to man; but God is faithful, who will not allow you to be tempted beyond what you are able, but with the temptation will also make the way of escape, that you may be able to bear it."

God gives you His guarantee that there is no such thing as a sin you *must* commit. He always provides you with the ability to flee temptation before you act. If this were not true, then God could rightly be accused of putting man in a catch-22, where He declared an act to be sinful that He knew people could not help but commit. If homosexuality was an inherited trait, then a person could no more help his sexual inclinations than he could change the location of his birth. For God to impugn someone who had no ability to refuse an action He deemed to be sinful would be tantamount to the idea that God takes pleasure in condemning humanity.

This goes against everything Scripture teaches about Yahweh's character, as He desires for all men to pursue righteousness (Gen. 6:5-6; Deut. 5:28-29; Isa. 48:17-18; Ezek. 33:11; Matt. 23:37). For God to set man up for failure by demanding something from him that would be impossible for him to achieve, and then to irrevocably condemn him for it, neither squares with Scripture nor passes the test of simple logic.

Do not misunderstand me. Man is a sinner by birth, by nature, and by choice, but technically speaking he does not "have to sin." James 1:13 says: "Let no one say when he is tempted, 'I am tempted by God'; for God cannot be tempted by evil, nor does He Himself tempt anyone." In regard to this last phrase, that God does not tempt anyone, John MacArthur explains: "God purposes trials to occur and in them He allows temptation to happen, but He has promised not to allow more than believers can endure and never without a way to escape (I Cor. 10:13). They choose whether to take the escape God provides or to give in."[1]

Let me send you to the bottom of the chute. God cannot ever be blamed for man's failure to say no to temptation. If anyone had ever been born with the inherent need to live as a homosexual, then God would not have a legitimate right to demand that such a person live a holy and sinless life. No man in history, other than the Lord Jesus, has ever lived a perfect life. As a result, every man needs Jesus to save him. The fatal flaw of the argument is not whether a man is correctly defined as a "sinner," but from whence the desire to commit sin originated. Since God is not the author of our sin, He can and does have every right to demand perfection from every person.

If what the homosexual lobby alleges about having been "born this way" were true, God's hand would be forced. One possibility is that He would have to make an exception for homosexuals (since they have no choice but to live in their sin) and give them a free pass into heaven, which would be unfair for everyone else whose sins are different from the homosexuals'. A second option would be to send all people who've ever committed a homosexual act to their doom, even if they'd accepted Jesus as their Savior, which would be unfair to the homosexuals because now theirs would be an unpardonable sin.

By the way, read I Cor. 6:9-11, and you will see that God Himself declares that homosexuals can and do come out of their sin. Verse 11 says that the pet sins of those listed in vs. 9-10 (a list that is partly comprised of a variety of sexual sins, including homosexuality) have been overcome by the blood of Jesus in the lives of those who had received Him. God says that there is no sin so terrible that He can't cleanse you of it or get you out of it.

A third alternative would be for God to declare that homosexuality is not a sin. If that were the case, then God would have to change His mind, which has never happened and never will. (See Num. 23:19; I Sam. 15:29; Psalm 102:26-27; Mal. 3:6; Tit. 1:2; Heb. 6:18.) I can think of no act mentioned in the Bible, apart from the rejection of Jesus and His sacrifice, that is more clearly stated as being a sin than the sin of homosexuality. If God were to retract His position on this, it would call into serious question the idea that such a thing as sin even exists.

No, there is only one right answer here, and it is obvious: Homosexuality is a sin, period. Like any sin, it can be avoided. Like any sin, it is forgivable. Like any sin, it demands repentance. Failure to act accordingly will be met with severe and eternal punishment handed down by a holy and perfect God.

21

LOOKING FOR A WAY OUT

I could go on and on in my bid to show all that is wrong with the societal acceptance of sexual perversion, but if all the evidence you've read up to now hasn't persuaded you, then in all likelihood your ignorance is invincible. Therefore, I will end this section of the book with just a few random thoughts.

Lamech never understood the purpose of marriage. He proved that when he took his second wife. The only way Lamech could justify bigamy was to assume that his marriage was about *him*. If you go back and read I Cor. 7:1-5, 10-16; Eph. 5:22-33; Col. 3:18-19; I Pet. 3:1-7, there is a theme that repeatedly keeps popping up: Marriage is not about you. Of the multitude of things that is wrong with the societal approval of homosexuality, chief among them is that God forbids it.

The second biggest reason not to endorse it is that its supporters make the crucial mistake of assuming that marriage is a manmade creation designed for self-gratification. Nothing could be further from the truth. Marriage was designed by God and is meant to glorify Him. Furthermore, marriage (as we see in the aforementioned verses) is about putting your spouse ahead of yourself. One of the many reasons why homosexual households are inherently dysfunctional is because the parties involved are in the relationship for what they can get out of it.

The homosexual relationship has as its centerpiece – drum roll please – sex. Homosexuals are loudly demanding their rights to marry, and they say it's because they, like heterosexuals, have a "right to be happy." But God is not interested in our happiness; He is concerned about our holiness. As for homosexual relationships, the outstanding unique element of such a union is the nature of the acts of intimacy. Homosexuals desire relationships with the same sex in order to satisfy their own sexual appetites (Rom. 1:27).

Whatever else can be said about homosexuality, the argument against it would be incomplete if no mention were made of the fact that what homosexuals do is <u>not</u> sex. The act of sex has only one definition: it is the physical union of one man and one woman. Nothing else qualifies.

Sexual fulfillment, properly understood, is the result of a loving marriage relationship. It is not the cause of the relationship. Any attempt to deviate from the one man/one woman paradigm automatically inverts the place of sexuality, making the physical act the central focus of the relationship. This, in turn, places the emphasis of importance on the self rather than the other person. Again, this is where Lamech's home broke down. He was interested only in what he could get, when his priority should have been on giving.

I'm going to close this section of the book with a true story. For several years, I was a Probation and Parole Officer for the State of Oklahoma. One of the people I supervised was a young man who was a homosexual; let's call him "Mike" (not his real name). The year was 1990, around Thanksgiving, if I remember right. I was 26 years of age, as was he. I was just starting out, still something of a newlywed, having been married only a couple of years.

Meanwhile, Mike's life was on a different trajectory. He had contracted AIDS through homosexual activity, and he would die soon. He was on probation for a drug possession charge, but he wouldn't live long enough to finish out his sentence. I remember Mike well. He was intelligent, friendly, well-spoken, humorous, and always courteous. But it didn't take me long to get to know a side of Mike that few people would ever see. He was sad – perhaps melancholy is a more descriptive term – and he was very, very lonely.

I guess Mike and I shared a special bond; he was open with me about many things. The last time I would ever see him was in my office two weeks before he died. I sat quietly and listened as Mike shared some parting thoughts with me. He told me that he could feel the pneumonia coming back. He said that pneumonia was a frequent companion of HIV patients, and he'd had it several times since he was diagnosed. He said he knew that the outcome would be different this time. "I've had it (pneumonia) once too often. My body is worn out, and I'm not able to fight it off anymore."

I honestly don't remember if Mike said he was afraid of dying, but I do remember some things he said about his life. "Ted," he whispered, "I wish that someone had been there for me when I was in high school. I wish someone could have pulled me aside and told me, 'There's a way out, Mike. You don't have to live like this.' The drugs, the partying, all the different lovers. It's part of the lifestyle. But I'm miserable. I never wanted any of this for my life. It's a terrible, destructive way to live. If only someone had been there to tell me that I had a choice. I hate the homosexual lifestyle. I hate that my decisions are what's going to kill me, but not any more than I hate the lifestyle itself. It never brought me anything but despair."

Were those Mike's exact words? No. That conversation took place 25 years ago. But the content of what Mike told me is precise. I never shed tears over what Mike said, or over his death. It's not because I wasn't sad. I've thought about him off and on for 25 years, and every time he enters into my memory banks I feel the weight of a crushing, indescribable sorrow. I could never have been the one to tell Mike, "You really don't have to live this way." I wasn't saved until the spring of 1997, more than six years after he died. I couldn't share with Mike the way out of his sin because I didn't know it myself.

There's nothing I can do to help Mike now, but I can do something about people who are shackled by their sin today. I can tell them about a Savior who died on a cross and was brought out of the grave three days later. I can tell them about that Savior, who ascended into heaven, who now sits at the right hand of God the Father. I can tell them that this Savior is coming again, this time for the salvation of those who eagerly await His return (Heb. 9:28).

With God's help, that is what I intend to do. I will not, I dare not, offer words of support for anyone who is imprisoned by their sin. To do so would be to make myself complicit in their evil deeds, which would serve a dual purpose. I would be sending them a mixed message, one that God never gave, and so confuse or mislead them that I would be guilty of bringing judgment upon them. At the same time, I would be bringing the wrath of God upon my own head (Ezek. 3:18-21). May God forbid I be found guilty of such a crime against my fellow man.

PART THREE

THE NONFUNCTIONING MIND

"And even as they did not like to retain God in their knowledge, God gave them over to a debased mind, to do those things which are not fitting; being filled with all unrighteousness, sexual immorality, wickedness, covetousness, maliciousness; full of envy, murder, strife, deceit, evil-mindedness; they are whisperers, backbiters, haters of God, violent, proud, boasters, inventors of evil things, disobedient to parents, undiscerning, untrustworthy, unloving, unforgiving, unmerciful" – Romans 1:28-31

22

AN INTRODUCTION TO A CULTURE OF DEATH

Romans 1:28 says that God gave the rebellious nation over to a "debased mind." That word "mind" is from the Greek "nous," and it means "intellect," "mind," or "understanding." That's straightforward enough. But take a long look at the word "debased." Consider the word and what you think its implications are. When you hear that word, what thoughts do you have? It's not a commonly used term these days, but it is highly descriptive and is full of meaning.

The Greek word for "debased" is "adokimos," and it's defined this way: "Not standing the test, rejected. Depraved, disqualified, fail the test, rejected, unapproved, worthless." Now we're beginning to see the severity of God's judgment. Remember that what we're looking at in this book is the revealing of God's wrath (Rom. 1:18), and in this third section we'll be examining the very late stages of His chastisement.

Paul has written, in the most literal sense conceivable, that God will finally give the people what they want. The first step man takes when he turns away from God is to willfully refuse to glorify Him (v. 21). Coinciding with that action is a posture of thanklessness. This leads to the "darkening" of the heart, which is to say that the people lose their ability to hear the Lord.

Then, in vs. 22-23, they make the treacherous decision to replace their worship of God with the worship of His creation. Then, after a while, they turn that worship toward themselves and at the same time they get more aggressive in their rejection of truth in favor of error (vs. 24-25). The stage to follow is sexual perversion and all that goes with it (vs. 26-27).

Now we come to the next phase of God's judgment, "the mind that fails the test." A debased mind is a mind that is disqualified. It is a mind that is rejected or unapproved. If minds were manufactured on an assembly line, the guy in charge of quality control would test these "debased" minds, put a "rejected" sticker on them, and throw them in the trash. The debased mind is a worthless mind, a mind that simply does not operate.

Hold onto this thought, and take a short detour with me. We'll come back to our exposition of the Scripture in a few minutes. Before I tell you what I'm going to tell you, you need to know that what you're about to read may be a bit disconcerting. However, it is completely true and unembellished. Feel free to check my sources.

Now that I've taken care of my disclaimer, let's get down to business. Do you remember the 2012 Democratic

National Convention? It was held in Charlotte, N.C. from September 4th through 6th. Among other things, they made public their official Democratic Party Platform, which was given the title "Moving America Forward." I am going to select a few choice quotes from that document. As you read them, keep in the front of your mind that these are the official positions of the Democratic Party for the presidential election year of 2012. Ready?

> "We believe in an America where everybody gets a fair shot and everybody plays by the same set of rules. At the core of the Democratic Party is the principle that no one should face discrimination on the basis of race, ethnicity, national origin, language, religion, gender, sexual orientation, gender identity, or disability status.
>
> "President Obama and the Democratic Party are committed to ensuring all Americans are treated fairly. This administration hosted the first-ever White House Conference on Bullying Prevention and we must continue our work to prevent vicious bullying of the young people and support LGBT youth. The President's record, from ending 'Don't Ask, Don't Tell' in full cooperation with our military leadership, to passing the Matthew Shepard and James Byrd Jr. Hate Crimes Prevention Act, to ensuring same-sex couples can visit each other in the hospital, reflects Democrats' belief that all Americans deserve the same chance to pursue happiness, earn a living, be safe in their communities, serve their country, and take care of the ones they love. The Administration has said that the word 'family' in immigration

includes LGBT relationships in order to protect bi-national families threatened with deportation.

"The Democratic Party strongly and unequivocally supports Roe v. Wade and a woman's right to make decisions regarding her pregnancy, including a safe and legal abortion, regardless of ability to pay. We oppose any and all efforts to weaken or undermine that right. Abortion is an intensely personal decision between a woman, her family, her doctor, and her clergy; there is no place for politicians or government to get in the way. We also recognize that health care and education help reduce the number of unintended pregnancies and thereby also reduce the need for abortions.

"We support the right of all families to have equal respect, responsibilities, and protections under the law. We support marriage equality and support the movement to secure equal treatment under law for same-sex couples. We also support the freedom of churches and religious entities to decide how to administer marriage as a religious sacrament without government interference.

"We oppose discriminatory federal and state constitutional amendments and other attempts to deny equal protection of the laws to committed same-sex couples who seek the same respect and responsibilities as other married couples. We support the full repeal of the so-called Defense of Marriage Act and the passage of the Respect for Marriage Act.

"We know that global climate change is one of the biggest threats of this generation – an economic, environmental, and national security catastrophe in the making. We affirm the science of climate change, commit to significantly

> reducing the pollution that causes climate change, and know we have to meet this challenge by driving smart policies that lead to greater growth in clean energy generation and result in a range of economic and social benefits.
>
> "The national security threat from climate change is real, urgent, and severe. The change wrought by a warming planet will lead to new conflicts over refugees and resources; new suffering from drought and famine; catastrophic natural disasters; and the degradation of vital ecosystems across the globe."[1]

As you can see, we have an entire political party here in America that has given its decisive and unambiguous support to the very sins we find in Romans 1. Whether we're talking about "saving the planet" (aka the worship of creation rather than the Creator), unnatural sexuality, or abortion, the Democratic Party of these United States made it abundantly plain that they were going to come down on the devil's side on every one of these major issues. I can just hear the objections now: "The Republicans aren't any better!" "The Democrats do a lot of good!" "My grandpa was a Democrat, and he's in heaven now, so just back off!"

To those out there lining up to give me the what-for, let me calmly say, "Hold the phone. Give me a minute more." First, what you just read is a direct quote from the 2012 Democratic Party platform. Second, "Lamech's Rebellion" is not a book about politics; it is a book about sin. Third, I am not by any means trying to sell anyone the idea that the Republican Party or the Independent Party or the Green Party or the Tea Party or the Communist Party or the Slumber Party are any better. Frankly, I've had it up to here with the abuses and the mendacity of pretty much everybody in just about every corner of our government. The problem is not the Constitution. Properly understood and correctly employed, the U.S. Constitution could be the catalyst for a wonderful form of government and a free and prosperous society. I know this to be true because there was a day when that was indeed the case.

But this book is not a commentary on the Democrats, the Republicans, or even the Constitution. I have written what you're reading here in Chapter 22 because I want you to understand just how far along we are on God's disciplinary scale. And since I've opened this smelly can of worms, I may as well finish what I've started. We haven't explored the dark caverns of abortion yet, but that's where we're going next. This section of the book will be devoted primarily to the violence that saturates an impious people. I know of nothing more violent than the grisly methods used by so-called doctors who make their living by destroying the most helpless and innocent of all human beings. So fasten your seatbelts; we're in for a bumpy night.

23

BOOING GOD, HAILING SATAN

Lamech, you will recall, was the first bigamist. He was also a murderer, following in the footsteps of Cain. I suppose it could be argued that Lamech acted in self-defense, since all we have to go on is Lamech's side of the story. Remember what he said in Gen. 4:23-24, about the man he killed for striking him? He was also the first recorded person to use the "He hit me first!" argument.

Lamech's word doesn't mean much, though. He was married to two women at the same time, so he clearly was preeminently occupied with himself and what he wanted. He had no understanding of who God was, and he had no desire for a relationship with Him. Lamech cared only for what he could take from his two wives, just as he cared only for the blessings and protection that he believed God owed to him. Sorry, Lamech, but your credibility in the eyes of the Court stands at nil.

Lamech believed that all he needed to do to get what he wanted from the Lord was just snap his fingers. It worked on his two wives, so why wouldn't it work that way with God? That's exactly how the crafters of the aforementioned Democratic platform saw it. They made all sorts of vile claims and, in the very same document, invoked the holy name of the Lord God. A United

Methodist pastor stood up during the convention's proceedings and made a motion for two amendments to be added to the platform. Here they are: "Amendment 1: Page 32, Line 48: We need a government that stands up for the hopes, values, and interests of working people, and gives everyone willing to work hard the chance to make the most of their God-given potential. Amendment 2: Page 63, Line 26: Jerusalem is and will remain the capital of Israel. The parties have agreed that Jerusalem is a matter for final status negotiations. It should remain an undivided city accessible to people of all faiths."[1]

The delegates were then asked to vote on the amendments, with the explanation given by the Master of Ceremonies that a two-thirds voice vote in the affirmative was necessary in order to carry the motion. The first vote clearly didn't garner the required majority, and in fact it barely sounded like a majority at all. The emcee took a second vote, and the results were the same. Evidently, the Democratic National Committee wanted the motion to pass, so the emcee declared that there was a clear two-thirds majority and that the amendments would be added. Immediately after his announcement, the arena erupted in boos, hissing, and catcalls. The people BOOED God, and they booed Israel, the covenant people of God.[2]

A written analysis of this unbelievable scene was posted beneath the referenced YouTube video. It reads: "At 2012 Democrat (sic) National Convention, DNC Chair Antonio

Villaraigosa holds three votes on the reinserting references to 'God' and 'Jerusalem' back into Democratic Party platform. The language had been removed from the 2012 Democrat Party platform, igniting a firestorm of criticism but reflective of the Obama administration's often lukewarm support for Israel and the President's omission of references to 'God' from his readings of the Declaration of Independence. The DNC Chair tries three times to secure the required two-thirds floor vote to change the DNC platform to reinsert the references to God and Jerusalem, but a majority of the Democrat delegates clearly vote each time against the platform change.

"Finally, the DNC Chair gives up, cynically declares that two-thirds of the delegates have voted for the platform change, and the motion passes. The delegates boo in disapproval of the reinsertion of God and Jerusalem back into the Democratic platform, and the display of Obama-style Chicago politics at work."[3]

Regardless of whether or not you recollect this deplorable event, please find the video and watch it; it lasts only 3-1/2 minutes. Afterward, you can go to a couple more YouTube videos I need to mention. In June, 2013, Texas state legislator Wendy Davis stood on the House floor and filibustered for eleven straight hours in an attempt to thwart a vote on Texas Senate Bill 5. This bill calls for a ban on all abortions after 20 weeks of pregnancy, it requires abortionists to provide admitting privileges to a hospital near the abortion clinic, and it requires all abortion clinics to meet the standards that hospitals must meet.[4]

Mrs. Davis's crusade fell short, and the legislature voted to pass the bill. About a week after this spectacle, crowds of people on both sides of the abortion debate descended on the State Capitol building in a show of solidarity for their side of the argument. While a woman from the pro-life camp gave a short speech of exhortation and personal testimony, those on the pro-abortion side tried to drown her out with loud chants of "Hail, Satan!"[5] At another point during the clash, pro-lifers began to sing "Amazing Grace." The pro-abortion supporters countered with their own hymn, another stanza of "Hail, Satan!"[6]

As repugnant as this is, I at least appreciate the fact that the people on the pro-abortion side of this issue are acknowledging the true point of origin for the killing of the unborn. I will be devoting the next several chapters to giving you an apologetic for why every person ought to be pro-life. As you read, keep these words of Jesus to His opponents in the front of your mind: "You are of your father the devil, and the desires of your father you want to do. He was a murderer from the beginning, and does not stand in the truth, because there is no truth in him. When he speaks a lie, he speaks from his own resources, for he is a liar and the father of it" (John 8:44).

24

KILLERS ON THE LOOSE

For just a moment, I need to turn your attention back to the 2012 Democratic Party platform. The Party's position on abortion bears repeating. It states: "The Democratic Party strongly and unequivocally supports Roe v. Wade and a woman's right to make decisions regarding her pregnancy, including a safe and legal abortion, regardless of ability to pay. We oppose any and all efforts to weaken or undermine that right. Abortion is an intensely personal decision between a woman, her family, her doctor, and her clergy; there is no place for politicians or government to get in the way. We also recognize that health care and education help reduce the number of unintended pregnancies and thereby also reduce the need for abortions."[1]

The protesters in Texas paid proper homage to the devil, proper in the sense that the devil is the one who invented and most vigorously promotes the homicidal practice we call abortion. Just as the protesters correctly identified Satan and his role, so, too, did the drafters of the Party's platform give us insight into the <u>real</u> purpose of abortion. In the last sentence of the above quote, the authors of the document reveal that the need for abortion is directly tied to "unintended pregnancies." This can and does mean only one thing: Abortion is nothing more and nothing less than birth control. It is not for the "health of the mother." Abortion has nothing whatsoever to do with women's health. It has always been exclusively used as a cruel and violent means of birth control, and the Democratic Party platform provides inarguable proof of this fact.

We live in an era where words and their meanings are ceaselessly up for grabs, but what I found in the Democratic platform on this matter of abortion is not vague in any way. Barack Obama has certainly made it plain through all of his words and actions that he, like the party's platform, rests on the farthest edges of the radical pro-abortion movement. On March 29, 2008, during his first campaign for president, Obama said that he's going to teach his two young daughters "...about values and morals, but if they make a mistake, I don't want them punished with a baby."[2]

Before anyone leaps out of his recliner to rescue Obama and try to parse these words of his, please allow me two more quotes from his lips. As he stood at a lectern and addressed a crowd of Planned Parenthood employees and supporters, then-presidential candidate Obama made this chilling statement about abortion: "There will always be people, many of good will, who do not share my view on the issue of choice. On this fundamental issue, I will not yield, and Planned Parenthood will not yield." Later in that same speech, Obama answered a spectator's question about “anti-choice legislation with this comment: “Well, the first thing I’d do as president is sign the Freedom of Choice Act.”[3]

Finally, Obama summarizes his romance with Planned Parenthood’s gruesome mission of wholesale infanticide. In a more recent speech to Planned Parenthood and abortion activists, Obama spoke these words: “That’s why no matter how great the challenge, no matter how fierce the opposition, there’s one thing the past few years have shown. It’s that Planned Parenthood is not going anywhere. It’s not going anywhere today, it’s not going anywhere tomorrow. As long as we’ve gotta fight to make sure women have access to quality, affordable health care, and as long as we’ve got to fight to protect a woman’s right to make her own choices about her own health, I want you to know that you’ve also got a president who’s gonna be right there with you, fighting every step of the way. Thank you, Planned Parenthood. God bless you, and God bless America.”[4]

It’s obvious that Obama has hitched his wagon promoting women’s health to Planned Parenthood and its commitment to “the issue of choice.” The follow-up question, then, is “Just how committed to abortion is Planned Parenthood?” If you go to plannedparenthood.org, which is their website, you can see for yourself how resolute this federally funded bureaucracy is when it comes to killing children. Their website is overflowing with information and persuasive advertisements that give praise to abortion.

Another of Planned Parenthood's websites gives a little rundown of their objectives regarding abortion. This is what they say on their homepage about abortion access: "Planned Parenthood believes every woman should have access to the full range of reproductive health care services, including access to safe and legal abortion. Our primary goal is prevention – reducing the number of unintended pregnancies. While teen pregnancy rates have declined significantly since 1990, the number of repeat teen birth rates remains high and we still have a lot of work to do. That's why it is important that every woman have access to affordable birth control, so she can choose and consistently use the method that works for her. At the same time, decisions about whether to choose adoption, end a pregnancy, or raise a child must be left to a woman, her family, and her faith, with the counsel of her doctor or health care provider – not to politicians.

"Access to abortion is legal, constitutionally protected, and consistently supported by a majority of Americans; yet anti-women's health policymakers have made it increasingly hard for women to access through court battles, ballot measures, and burdensome legislative restrictions on abortion services. Some extremists even resort to intimidation, harassment, and violence against women and health care providers.

"Planned Parenthood fights these efforts on every level. From courthouses to statehouses to Capitol Hill to the grassroots, we work to protect access to reproductive health care through education of elected officials, litigation, and mobilization of more than seven million Planned Parenthood activists, donors, supporters, and patients."[5]

There should be no mystery as to where America's chief executive stands in regard to the matter of killing the unborn. But this is not a book about just one man, not even the president. This book is about the sinfulness of our town, our state, our nation, and our world. Again, my goal is to equip you to identify sins that have spread throughout the land like a cancer and how we as Christians are to "refuse to yield" under constantly mounting pressure to conform.

25

ROE VS. LIFE

I'm not a scientist, but I know the tactics of people who want to win an argument (be it scientific or otherwise) when they know they're wrong. An attorney who has the facts on his side will argue the facts. An attorney who has the law on his side will argue the law. An attorney who has neither on his side will attack the witness. This is how we know that climate change alarmists have a weak argument. Just like Darwinian evolutionists, they appeal to the last resort; they try to attack, belittle, and silence anyone who dares to speak against them. These next few chapters will be spent covering the facts, the law, and the witnesses of the abortion debate.

We've already heard from the pro-abortion camp, which, as you surely know by now, is poured from Lamech's mold. Lamech gave no thought to his polygamous lifestyle, his fiendish disposition, or his contrived relationship with God. The exact same things can be said about proponents of infanticide. Lamech saw no conflict between his practice of sexual sin and his invoking of God's name to demand divine protection. He saw no harm in murdering someone who had inconvenienced him, and he erroneously believed that this would not alter his standing before the Judge of the universe. Abortion, which is usually the direct result of sexual sin, is designed to kill a person who has inconvenienced another. Those doing the killing either believe that God is unconcerned with their nefarious acts (which was played out in the 2012 Democratic Party platform), or they sneer at the Lord and deliberately mock Him (as we saw with Texas legislator Wendy Davis, the demonstrators chanting "Hail, Satan," and the people who booed God at the Democratic Convention).

Can I insert another thought here, a thought about booing God? I believe the Democratic Party would have been better off leaving God out of their platform. To promote the opprobrious, malevolent things that awful document promoted, and then to somehow try and tie them to our great God as though He would approve, is blasphemy.

As another little detour, here's another little morsel of food for thought. When all of the fluff and misdirection is stripped away, the advocate of abortion has three arguments: (1) That the person inside his mother's womb is not really a person; (2) That the person in the womb may be destroyed for the sake of convenience; and (3) That the person in the womb may be used for the sake of financial gain. These three arguments are identical to the case that was once made in this country in support of slavery. The slaveholder would say that his slaves were: (1) Not human; (2) His personal property to do with as he pleased, including destroy them for the sake of convenience; and (3) His to use or abuse for the sake of profit.

Okay, now that I got that off my chest, we'll look first at the laws regarding abortion. Obviously, supporters of abortion have the law on their side. I find it significant that the pro-abortion lobby seldom uses the law to support their view. (The reasons for this should become apparent as we travel through this minefield.)

The Trojan horse of abortion in the U.S. is, naturally, the Roe v. Wade ruling of 1973. There are several facets of the Roe decision, but it was a watershed moment because it invalidated all limitations placed on abortions during the first trimester of pregnancy.[1]

Using a novel interpretation of the ninth and fourteenth amendments to the U.S. Constitution, Roe's effects could be summarized this way: "In the first trimester, the state (that is, any government) could treat abortion only as a medical decision, leaving medical judgment to the woman's physician. In the second trimester (before viability), the state's interest was seen as legitimate when it was protecting the health of the mother. After viability of the fetus (the likely ability of the fetus to be able to survive outside and separated from the uterus), the *potential* of human life could be considered as a legitimate state interest, and the state could choose to 'regulate or even proscribe abortion' as long as the life and health of the mother was protected."[2]

To reduce Roe to its skeleton, it made abortion during the first three months of pregnancy legal on demand in all 50 states. The fourth through ninth months were put up for grabs based on the viability of the child and the health of the mother. On its face, this law doesn't sound too bad, so long as you accept the statement that a baby in his mother's womb constitutes merely a potential for life and not an actual life. This is where the Roe decision breaks down, because it fails to recognize the fact that life begins at conception.

I will prove this fact in pages to come, but first I have to address another fatal flaw in Roe, a flaw that might be less visible but is just as serious. Because the Court failed to accurately pinpoint when life begins, it ripped the proverbial lid to Pandora's Box off its hinges. If life begins at any point beyond conception, when exactly does it begin? And who has the wherewithal to make that determination? With the Roe decision, the Court emphatically stated that life begins sometime after the first trimester of pregnancy.

I say "emphatic" because the Court made it mandatory for all states to provide abortion on demand at any point during the first 90 days of pregnancy. This inherently means that the Court did not recognize the baby as being "alive" during these earliest days of gestation. However, if it can be shown that the baby is alive during the first trimester, then the Court made the crime of murder legal in the U.S.A. To be clear, I am most definitely accusing the U.S. Supreme Court of that very thing, the sanctioning of murder in the first degree.

We need to exhaust this issue of when the Court says life begins, because: (a) It is the foundation of the Roe decision; and (b) It has led to even more egregious legal decisions. The first fatal flaw in Roe was its failure to acknowledge that life begins at conception. This flaw led to the second defect in the Court's judgment, which was its failure to determine when life does begin.

If life begins at any point in the first 90 days of pregnancy, Roe is inarguably advocating a murderous act. If life begins at some point after the conclusion of the first trimester, when does life begin? Since the Court failed to satisfactorily answer this, we now have other problems to wrestle with, like partial-birth abortion and late-term abortion. We will look behind the black curtain that hides the abortion clinics when we get to the witnesses, but I want to give you one witness's testimony here.

Since the abortion lobby still has the law on its side, and since the Supreme Court in 1973 failed in its mission to protect "life, liberty, and the pursuit of happiness," the ruling on Roe gave us witnesses like abortionist Martin Haskell and his nurse, Brenda Pratt Shafer. Mrs. Shafer, a registered nurse from Dayton, Ohio, testified before the U.S. Senate Judiciary Committee in November of 1995 about a partial-birth abortion on a woman who was more than 6-1/2 months pregnant. Mrs. Shafer had assisted abortionist Haskell in this act, the details of which were summarized and published.

Here is the summary of what she told the Senate Committee: "According to nurse Shafer, the baby was alive and moving as the abortionist 'delivered the baby's body and arms – everything but the head. The doctor kept the baby's head just inside the uterus. The baby's little fingers were clasping and unclasping, his feet were kicking. Then the doctor stuck the scissors through the back of his head, and the baby's arms jerked out in a flinch, a startle reaction, like a baby does when he thinks he might fall. The doctor opened up the scissors, stuck a high-powered suction tube into the opening and sucked the baby's brains out. Now the baby was completely limp.'"[3]

The article I just quoted also reported a tape-recorded statement made by Martin Haskell, who admitted that "...the majority of fetuses aborted this way (partial birth abortion) are alive until the end of the procedure."[4]

Did Haskell's admission or his nurse's testimony put an end to late-term abortion? A news article from over 16 years later gives us this answer: "The Ohio health department has updated an arrangement that allows late-term abortion practitioner Martin Haskell to continue doing abortions without following state law requiring him to have a transfer agreement at a local hospital. In 1996, Ohio passed a law requiring that all ambulatory surgical centers must be licensed by the state and, in 1999, it came to the attention of the Ohio Health Department that abortion clinics were not in compliance with the law, having never applied for licensing. The OHD began the process of insuring (sic) that all abortion clinics came into compliance.

"Haskell refused to comply and, after years of court and administrative battles, the administration of former Ohio governor Ted Strickland granted a variance [exception] allowing the late-term abortion practitioner to open a new abortion facility in Sharonville, Ohio... The state gave him this variance on the condition that he maintains privileges at an area hospital, a lesser standard than a transfer agreement."[5]

It wasn't until mid-2014 that Haskell's clinic was finally shut down due to his failure to comply with the mandatory written transfer agreement with a local hospital to cover patient emergencies.[6] Even with the harrowing testimony given by Martin Haskell's nurse, and even with the confession by Haskell that most of his abortions were performed on babies that were alive until the very end of the abortion, and even after the leniency shown to Haskell by the Ohio courts so that he had fewer restrictions on his clinic, and even though Haskell fought tooth-and-claw against these token regulations, it still took the State of Ohio nearly 20 years to shut down his slaughterhouse. We have Roe v. Wade to thank for that, and it's all because seven judges couldn't figure out when life begins. And we've barely scratched the surface of the aftermath of this terrible ruling.

26

FROM HIPPOCRATES TO HYPOCRITES

Hippocrates, who lived ca. 460-375 B.C., was a Greek physician who is widely regarded as the father of medicine. Today, his name lives on in what is called the Hippocratic Oath. This oath is used as a code of ethics for the medical profession; it is often recited in medical schools during commencement exercises.[1]

This oath, which can be traced to about 400 B.C., was translated into English from the Greek by one Francis Adams in 1849. It reads:

> "I swear by Apollo the physician, and Aesculapius, and Health, and All-heal, and all the gods and goddesses, that, according to my ability and judgment, I will keep this Oath and this stipulation – to reckon him who taught me this Art equally dear to me as my parents, to share my substance with him, and relieve his necessities if required; to look upon his offspring in the same footing as my own brother, and to teach them this art, if they shall wish to learn it, without fee or stipulation; and that by precept, lecture, and every other mode of instruction, I will impart a knowledge of the Art to my own sons, and those of my teachers, and to disciples bound by a stipulation and oath according to the law of medicine, but to none others. I will follow that system of

regimen which, according to my ability and judgment, I consider for the benefit of my patients, and abstain from whatever is deleterious and mischievous. I will give no deadly medicine to any one if asked, nor suggest any such counsel; and in like manner I will not give to a woman a pessary to produce abortion. With purity and with holiness I will pass my life and practice my Art. I will not cut persons laboring under the stone, but will leave this to be done by men who are practitioners of this work. Into whatever houses I enter, I will go into them for the benefit of the sick, and will abstain from every voluntary act of mischief and corruption; and, further from the seduction of females or males, of freemen and slaves. Whatever, in connection with my professional practice or not, in connection with it, I see or hear, in the life of men, which ought not to be spoken of abroad, I will not divulge, as reckoning that all such should be kept secret. While I continue to keep this Oath unviolated, may it be granted to me to enjoy life and the practice of the art, respected by all men, at all times. But should I trespass and violate this Oath, may the reverse be my lot."[2]

The oath has undergone a number of changes in recent years, and its current version bears only a nominal resemblance to the original wording. One internet source shined a light on the most significant alterations. The report quoted a 1993 survey of 150 medical schools in the U.S. and Canada, which found that "...only 14 percent of modern oaths prohibit euthanasia, 11 percent hold covenant with a deity, 8 percent foreswear abortion, and a mere 3 percent forbid sexual contact with patients – all maxims held sacred in the classical version."[3]

To be sure, the most likely reason given for these recent modifications to the oath is in order to accommodate our ever-evolving culture and its mores. May I say to you that I see some mighty big problems with that kind of thinking? First off, societies the world over and throughout all of history are given to what I would call a permanent state of moral flux. This does not describe God, not even a little bit. God does not change (Num. 23:19; I Sam. 15:29; Psa. 102:26-27; Mal. 3:6; Heb. 13:8; Jas. 1:17). The best way to understand what the Bible means in the here and now is to find out what it meant when it was written. I, for one, take comfort in the knowledge that God is reliable and consistent. In a world where everything is in an enduring state of transition, God is able to keep His children anchored through His character and His Word.

It just so happens that, when it came to the writing of this very chapter, my timing was impeccable. While I'm penning these words, in July of 2015, there is an outcry from both the public at large as well as several politicians in Washington demanding an investigation into the abortion practices of Planned Parenthood. A number of videos have been surfacing over a period of weeks that show some of Planned Parenthood's most accomplished abortionists in various types of compromising positions.[4]

Deborah Nucatola, an abortionist and senior director of medical services for Planned Parenthood, is the "star" of a video made by undercover investigators who posed as potential buyers of discarded human organs for research purposes. As far as Nucatola understood, the people who interviewed and secretly recorded her were representatives of a human biologics company. The video shows Nucatola sitting in a restaurant, and she appears to be very relaxed as she dines with the investigators and describes in graphic detail the means by which the aborted babies' organs are harvested. Nucatola tells her "customers" that she and her fellow abortionists perform abortions in such a way that they're able to recover intact lungs, livers, hearts, and other organs before they finish the job and kill the baby.[5] By the way, the method of abortion used by Planned Parenthood sounds identical to the techniques employed during partial-birth abortions. The baby's head is kept in the birth canal until the desired organs have been removed, and only then is the baby destroyed by crushing the head.

One of the subjects Nucatola touches on is the partial-birth abortion law. She tells her prospective clients that "...the federal (partial-birth) abortion ban is a law, and laws are up to interpretation. So if I say on day one, I do not intend to do this, what ultimately happens doesn't matter." She says this because of 18 U.S. Code 1513, which says that partial-birth abortion is a federal felony punishable by up to two years in prison and/or a fine of up to $250,000. Furthermore, 1 U.S. Code 8 says that a baby extracted intact and alive during an abortion is "…a born-alive infant under federal law and any further action taken to kill him or her is homicide."[6]

I know I said earlier that the pro-abortion lobby has the law on their side. I also know that partial-birth abortion is a crime under federal law. The rub, though, is what Nucatola said: "The federal abortion ban is a law, and laws are up to interpretation." Consider my proposition in the previous chapter, where I stated that the Supreme Court fumbled the ball when they failed to accurately determine when life begins. Had the Court done its job right, had the Justices had their wits about them, ALL abortions would be illegal and Planned Parenthood and Deborah Nucatola would have to be doing something entirely different to make a living.

If a pagan Greek man with no ultrasound or modern technology at his disposal knew that abortion is murder, how come 21st century Americans can't figure it out?

27

FACTS ARE STUBBORN THINGS

Twisted though they are, most federal statues regulating abortion are either weak enough, vague enough, or "up to interpretation" enough that the abortion industry continues to flourish, now more than 40 years after Roe v. Wade. Just how lucrative is this macabre business? Well, in the period between the Roe decision and 2011, about 50 million abortions have been legally performed in the United States. This breaks down to more than 1.2 million abortions per year, or a little more than 3,300 per day.[1]

Abortion is especially profitable for Planned Parenthood. In 2006, for example, this federally funded monster performed nearly one of every four abortions, making it the largest provider of abortions in the nation.[2] Given the high – dare I say *staggering* – numbers of abortions performed by Planned Parenthood, it should come as no surprise that abortion services account for a third of their annual revenue.[3]

I could continue to peel back the layers of this rotten onion we call the abortion industry, but I don't know how long it would take me to reach the middle. I could let my research branch off into many dark recesses, places you'd never even dream were associated with abortion. One of those haunted corners is the known link between abortion and a dramatically increased risk in breast cancer. Incredibly, there is also a trail that leads from breast cancer fundraising groups to Planned Parenthood. (How ironic it is that abortion providers, who are a direct cause of breast cancer, are also filling their coffers by raising money to stop the very disease they help cause!) If you're interested in drilling to the bottom of this well, I'll give you a few internet resources in my bibliography to get you started.[4]

But if I'm going to stay on task, I'm duty-bound to wrap up the pro-abortion side of the ledger by making this one concise observation: As of the summer of 2015, the pro-abortion lobby most definitely has the law on its side. One might think they would answer their critics with glib recitations of the law. They're unable to do that, though, because they're too busy putting out all the fires caused by the facts and the witnesses.

Many of the facts surrounding abortion are self-evident. One of the chief facts is that life must begin at conception. As we saw earlier, if life doesn't begin when the sperm fertilizes the egg, it must be determined what the criteria are for defining "life," and it must likewise be decided who gets to set those criteria. Then you have to decide who has the right to determine who gets to select the people who will be charged with the job of deciding who the people should be who will pick the people who get to decide when life begins. (You do see where this is going, yes?)

According to Scott Klusendorf, founder and president of Life Training Institute, there are four differences between a baby inside his mother's womb and a baby that has already been born. Those differences, which he compresses into the acronym "SLED," are: size, level of development, environment, and degree of dependency. Klusendorf argues that these are the only differences between the two groups (preborn and post-delivered babies), and none of the four differences – either individually or taken as a whole – disqualifies the preborn infant from being defined as a "person." (For more information on Klusendorf and his ministry, visit his website at prolifetraining.com.)

The subject matter and tactics used to try and justify abortion seem limitless, and I don't want to get wrapped up in a never-ending battle with the pro-abortion lobby about peripheral issues. There is only one question that needs to be answered in the abortion debate, and it is this: Is a child in his mother's womb a human being, or is he not? Klusendorf resoundingly answers that question in the affirmative, and he does so using solid reasoning and time-tested science. Therefore, I will leave this portion of the research up to you, and we shall turn our attention toward the next complainant against abortion, the Word of God.

28

THE SILENT WITNESS

Lamech did not treat human life with the kind of respect that God demands because Lamech did not have any respect for God. As evidenced by his bigamous lifestyle, Lamech valued women only for their utility to him. He gave no consideration to his wives' opinions or feelings. He wanted what he wanted, he got what he wanted, and for him that was all that he wanted.

Since Lamech was unconcerned about his own spouses, it comes as no surprise that he had no regard for people that were unrelated to him. As the horrific saga of Planned Parenthood continues to unfold while I pen these pages, what the world is able to see is the utter disregard that these clinics and so-called "doctors" have for human life. As the world looks on, one video after another is being released every few days by the Center for Medical Progress, a pro-life organization that has amassed considerable video evidence of the murderous practices of America's largest abortion provider.[1]

Lamech's first big sin was an act of rebellion against God's plan for the family. His second sin was his casual response to having murdered his fellow man. America's abortion industry found a way to commit the worst kind of murder, which is murder for profit. That was their first sin. This led to their second sin, which is a financial double-dipping on their tiny, helpless victims. We've known all along that abortionists get their paycheck by killing babies, but now we know that they pocket even more cash by salvaging organs and body parts and selling them to hospitals and universities.

This is how sin always works. There's an old potato chip commercial that ended with the slogan, "Nobody can eat just one." Sin is just like that. I John 1:9 says that "If we confess our sins, He is faithful and just to forgive us our sins and to cleanse us from all unrighteousness." The reason God commands that we confess our sins is so that we might acknowledge our actions as being an affront to Him. The first step toward true repentance always begins with our recognition of sin and our need to turn from it. If we refuse to admit our sin, then we will naturally turn further away from God and toward the sin. That's why God warned Cain that sin wants nothing more than to take over his life, and that it was incumbent upon Cain to achieve mastery over his sin lest his sin be successful in overtaking him (Gen. 4:7). We all know how that turned out. In the very next verse, Cain murdered his own brother.

So it was with Lamech, and so it is today with those who dare to maintain their unrepentant posture toward abortion. What a treacherous place it is when a man learns that he is in sin but hardens his heart against it. It must be the chore of every Christian to be in a continual battle against sin, because sin lies in wait at every doorstep, and its purpose is to first control and then destroy the sinner. The Christian's first line of defense against this insidious foe is confession.

What I've observed over the past few years is that when it comes to a subject of controversy, the battle lines keep getting drawn and redrawn because of newly discovered information. People are constantly chasing down new evidence to try and prove their own side, or they're plotting ways to trap their opponents and impeach their credibility. But the one thing that nobody wants to use is the one that everybody should use. Psalm 119:89 tells us that God has declared His word to be eternally settled; His word is the last word. The abortion war, which has raged in this country for over 40 years, has heated up even more in the year of our Lord 2015.

It is a sad commentary on the state of our union when we can't determine if a baby in his mother's womb is a person or not. While senators and congressmen and officers of the courts and even theologians are fumbling around and scratching their heads, trying to find an answer to this fundamental question, babies are still being yanked alive from their mother's bodies so they can be stripped of their internal organs like a car in a chop shop and then sold to the highest bidder.

On August 22, 2015, there was a nationwide protest against Planned Parenthood. Thousands of people showed up at these clinics all across the country in a synchronized effort to draw attention to the scourge of abortion. Debbie and I attended the rally here in our hometown of Oklahoma City, along with about 200 fellow protesters. The scene reminded me of Acts 17, where Paul preached to the men of Athens about the Lord Jesus and the resurrection from the dead. After presenting his hearers with the gospel, Paul closed up shop and departed. According to Acts 17:32-34, the audience fell into one of three categories: those who mocked, those who believed, and those who stayed on the fence ("We will hear you again on the matter" – v. 33).

Our band of demonstrators encountered those same three kinds of people. There were those who cheered us, and there were those who jeered us. (Both groups were equally enthusiastic in the voicing of their opinions. It looked a lot like the clash at the Texas State Capitol.) There was also a third group, and it was by far the most populous. Most people had nothing to say one way or the other. They drove or walked by with expressionless countenances. They would turn their heads in our direction, but they didn't really see us. This third group was the one that troubled me most. There is virtually no way that that many Americans didn't know about these terrible videos exposing Planned Parenthood, yet their reaction was one of total indifference. When it comes to the message of salvation, there is no worse position to be in than one of frigid neutrality. The same holds true for the message of the value of human life.

And all the while, standing quietly in the shadows where He's been pushed by a complacent society, is a holy and indignant Creator God, heaving sighs of sorrow and great anger. Why would He not be furious with us? Why would He not be readying Himself to pour out His fury full-strength on such a sinful generation? The reality is that the wheels of God's judgment, which have been turning for some time, will pick up speed as long as we persist in our rebellion. If we fail to turn away from our sin and back to the Lord, those wheels will grind us to powder.

29

THE WRITTEN WITNESS

It takes a debased mind, or, if you prefer, a nonfunctioning mind, to convince the person who possesses it that such vile acts can in any way be considered acceptable. If you are a Christian, you do not and cannot possess such a mind, for believers "have the mind of Christ" (I Cor. 2:16). It naturally follows, then, that Christians care more about what God says about a matter than what the whole entire world might say. To accept Jesus is to reject everything that opposes Him. To accept the Bible as truth is to reject everything that conflicts with it. If you don't believe that the Bible is true to the exclusion of all other books and beliefs, you are not a Christian. There have always been those who mock the Word of God. As long as they are "natural men" (I Cor. 2:10-16), they will refuse to believe the Bible. For the Christian, however, no other source comes close in importance.

In this chapter, I will lay out some key verses of Scripture that should help clarify and crystallize what God has to say about a country that has become a killing field for its unborn. Keep in mind the fact that between the Roe decision of 1973 and the summer of 2015 (the time of my writing of this chapter), there have been more than 58 million abortions in America. That breaks down to a rough estimate of 3,700 abortions every single day since 1973, which means that a little over 150 babies are killed in their mother's womb every hour in the U.S.[1]

For the record, between January 1, 2015 and August 2, 2015, abortionists completed more than 640,000 abortions on American soil; nearly 200,000 of those were done by Planned Parenthood.[2] By the way, fewer than 1% of all abortions in the U.S. are on babies conceived as a result of rape or incest.[3] As prolific as America has become at slaughtering its unborn, it's high time we ask the Author of all life what He thinks about this ghastly business.

In truth, the Bible says far more about the subject of abortion than one might think. Instead of exhausting every verse and passage that comes to my mind, I'm going to stick to the interstates and just give you some highlights. Let's begin with a pattern that is followed by a couple of evil men. The first such man was king over Egypt at a time when the Egyptians held the children of Israel captive. Israel was growing by leaps and bounds in terms of their population, and their increasing numbers alarmed the Egyptian people (Exo. 1:8-12). Because of the Egyptians' fear, they sought to overwhelm the Jews by oppressing them with hard labor. When their plan backfired, the king ordered the Hebrew midwives to kill all the male children born to the Jewish women. This plot failed as well, so Pharaoh went on to Plan C, which was to drown all the little Jewish boys (see Exo. 1:13-22).

Pharaoh was determined to kill off the Jews, and all his schemes revolved around the killing of the babies.

Our second celebrity from the Scriptures was a man named Herod. In Matt. 2:1-2, a group of Gentiles described as "wise men" arrived in Jerusalem in search of Israel's Messiah. This news greatly disturbed Herod, so he sought to destroy this new King (vs. 4-7, 12, 16). The end of Herod's plan, which was to murder all the male children two years old and younger throughout Bethlehem, sounds eerily similar to Pharaoh's strategy from about 1,500 years earlier.

Here's a question to ask anyone who persists in the mindset that a child in his mother's womb is not a human being: If whatever is being extracted from a woman's belly is not a person, what is it? Abortionists are successfully recovering hearts, lungs, livers, kidneys, brains, and all kinds of assorted tissues in order to sell them to a third party. The victim of an abortion, who possessed all of these organs before having them callously torn from his body, is defined by supporters of abortion as something other than human. If that creature wasn't a person, then what was it?

When he was confronted with the threat of a growing population among his captives, Pharaoh cried, "Kill the babies!" When he caught wind of the fact that a King – a potential usurper – had been born in his territory, Herod screamed, "Kill the babies!" When Communist China began to feel the pinch of its enormous population crushing the life out of an ill-conceived political system, the government had a solution: "Kill the babies!" When Americans, thanks to the sexual revolution, came to the realization that there was a price to be paid for their promiscuous ways, they picked up the refrain and began to shout, "Kill the babies!" It seems that the devil has always had a fondness for killing the young, the weak, and the helpless.

While we're on the subject of a mother's womb, below are several examples from Scripture that plainly teach us that life begins at conception. The first instance is well-known. In Jer. 1:5, God tells His young prophet that He "knew" Jeremiah before He formed him in his mother's womb. It's important to note that God *knew* the child before He created him, and *then* God did the creating (or "forming") of the child. This concept is given to us in intricate and explicit detail by David in Psalm 139:13-16: "For You formed my inward parts; You covered me in my mother's womb. I will praise You, for I am fearfully and wonderfully made; Marvelous are Your works, And that my soul knows very well. My frame was not hidden from You, When I was made in secret, And skillfully wrought in the lowest parts of the earth. Your eyes saw my substance, being yet unformed. And in Your book they all were written, The days fashioned for me, When as yet there were none of them."

The Psalms also have another highly potent statement about the moment life begins. In Psalm 51:5, the psalmist (David again) wrote that he was a sinner from the time of his conception. I have several other scriptural references to make, but I need to pause here long enough to point out that this single sentence is a touchstone that helps us understand everything more deeply. Prepare yourself for a crash course in knowing God and knowing His creation. Ready?

God is holy. Man is sinful. God has never been nor will He ever be anything but perfect in every way. From the time of the fall in Eden, man has never been anything but sinful. There are two things in all of God's creation (which includes heaven, hell, and the entire created universe) that are capable of sin: man and angels. Angels are disqualified from this colloquy because they've either already sinned and have become demons or they haven't sinned and they therefore never will. (For a thorough analysis of angels and demons, I recommend the book "Angels: God's Secret Agents," by Billy Graham.) That leaves us with only the human race. Only man can sin against God, ergo only man can rightly be called a sinner. If a sinner must be a person, and if God declares the thing that is conceived in a woman's womb as being a sinner, and if that thing was a sinner from the instant that it was conceived, then the sinful thing in mother's womb must be a person and he must have been a person at the time he was conceived.

There. That should explain a lot. God has never been anything but perfect and righteous and holy, while you and I have never had any of those traits, not even when we were *persons* being formed in our mother's belly.

The same type of argument can be made from Judges 13:2-5, where a woman from the tribe of Dan was told by a heavenly messenger that she would bear a son and name him Samson. She was instructed not to eat anything unclean or consume the fruit of the vine, because "...the child shall be a Nazirite to God from the womb..." (v. 5). Since a Nazirite can only be a person, and since Nazirites are not allowed to consume wine or beverages made from grapes (cf. Num. 6:1-8), and since Samson would be in violation of the Nazirite vow if his mother were to imbibe during the days of her pregnancy, there is but one reasonable conclusion: Samson was a *person* from the time that he was conceived.

In Luke 1:15, Zacharias is told by the angel Gabriel that his wife would soon bear a son (John the Baptist), and that he would be filled with the Holy Spirit from his mother's womb. Same sort of argument here, that only a *person* can be filled with the Holy Spirit of God. John was given the gift of the Spirit while he was still in the womb, which means that John was a person while God was yet forming him in the womb. The Spirit is what enabled John to recognize that he was in the presence of the Messiah, which is why he leaped for joy in his mother's womb upon hearing the voice of Mary (Luke 1:41,44). This also means that John had the ability to both hear and reason before he left the womb, and those are once again characteristics of a living person. Oh, yeah, there's also the matter of the Messiah. In Luke 1:42-43, Elizabeth (John's mother) recognized that Mary was carrying her Lord. The Lord Jesus was identified here as being a person, since the Messiah is also a person.

Finally, I want to take you to one more place in Scripture. Right on the heels of God having given Moses the Ten Commandments, the Lord dictated some various other laws. Among those were ordinances concerning violence, and one in particular stands out in regard to crimes against the unborn. It's found in Exo. 21:22-25: "If men fight, and hurt a woman with child, so that she gives birth prematurely, yet no harm follows, he shall surely be punished accordingly as the woman's husband imposes on him; and he shall pay as the judges determine. But if any harm follows, then you shall give life for life, eye for eye, tooth for tooth, hand for hand, foot for foot, burn for burn, wound for wound, stripe for stripe."

Once again, God couldn't make His position on this subject any clearer. Whatever harm comes to the child as a result of any injury inflicted on his mother during pregnancy, that same harm is to be put upon the perpetrator. Should the baby die, then "life for life;" it would be no different if the mother herself had been murdered. In God's eyes, the babe still being formed inside his mother's body is no less human than the mother herself.

Having now made my scriptural case, I wish to call a few witnesses to the stand. Prepare yourself, because I may call a surprise witness somewhere along the way.

30

THE HUMAN WITNESS

"When the team members entered the clinic, they were appalled, describing it to the Grand Jury as 'filthy,' 'deplorable,' 'disgusting,' 'very unsanitary, very outdated, horrendous,' and 'by far, the worst' that these experienced investigators had ever encountered. There was blood on the floor. A stench of urine filled the air. A flea-infested cat was wandering through the facility, and there were cat feces on the stairs. Semi-conscious women scheduled for abortions were moaning in the waiting room or the recovery room, where they sat on dirty recliners covered with blood-stained blankets. All the women had been sedated by unlicensed staff – long before Gosnell arrived at the clinic – and staff members could not accurately state what medications or dosages they had administered to the waiting patients. Many of the medications in inventory were past their expiration dates... surgical procedure rooms were filthy and unsanitary... resembling 'a bad gas station restroom.' Instruments were not sterile. Equipment was rusty and outdated. Oxygen equipment was covered with dust, and had not been inspected. The same corroded suction tubing used for abortions was the only tubing available for oral airways if assistance for breathing was needed...

"Fetal remains [were] haphazardly stored throughout the clinic – in bags, milk jugs, orange juice cartons, and even in cat-food containers... Gosnell admitted to Detective Wood that at least 10 to 20 percent...were probably older than 24 weeks [the legal limit]... In some instances, surgical incisions had been made at the base of the fetal skulls. The investigators found a row of jars containing just the severed feet of fetuses. In the basement, they discovered medical waste piled high. The intact 19-week fetus delivered by Mrs. Mongar three months earlier was in a freezer. In all, the remains of 45 fetuses were recovered... at least two of them, and probably three, had been viable."[1]

This excerpt was taken from just one of many lengthy documents pertaining to the case of Philadelphia abortionist Kermit Gosnell, who, in 2013, was convicted of murder, manslaughter, and performing late-term abortions. As repugnant as it was for me to read and then write about this man and his crimes, it got me to thinking. The medical industry is one of the most heavily regulated fields in the United States. I can't help but wonder how a clinic like this could continue to run for years – decades, actually – without somebody putting a stop to it. Thoughts like these make me wonder other things, too, like "How many more clinics around the country are like Gosnell's?" It's almost as if the government itself was in on the action...

Kermit Gosnell is perhaps an extreme example of the goings-on in abortion clinics in America, but he most assuredly has not acted alone for all these years since 1973. I realize that I've put you through the proverbial wringer over these past few chapters, so I believe it's time you were introduced to a few people who champion the cause of life.

Our first guest is Melissa Ohden. With a Master's in Social Work, Melissa has been active in disciplines related to mental health, but she is also a vocal opponent of abortion. Next is Sarah Smith. She and her mother travel all over the world and speak on the horrors of abortion. Then there's the heroic work of Gianna Jessen. Despite the fact that she has cerebral palsy, she, too, is an outspoken supporter of the right to life. She even spoke before the U.S. House Judiciary Committee in 1996.

Others whose names you should know include Dr. Imre Teglasy, Heidi Huffman, Claire Culwell, Carrie Holland-Fischer, Josiah Presley, and Hope Hoffman. Every one of these people shares a common bond in that they each participate in ministries that are seeking to end the holocaust of abortion. You see, the reason they've dedicated their lives to this vital cause is because they're all survivors of abortions. I urge you to read for yourself about these heroic people; their stories can be found online at theabortionsurvivors.com. That's the website for

The Abortion Survivors Network, which was founded by Melissa Ohden.

Every survivor of abortion is living proof that abortion is precisely what the pro-life lobby says it is. After all, if abortion isn't killing, then no one would survive an abortion.

All right, I teased you with the possibility of a surprise witness. Without further ado, here he is. Please give a warm welcome to Dr. Bernard Nathanson. Dr. Nathanson (1926-2011) was a New York abortionist and cofounder of NARAL, the National Association for the Repeal of Abortion Laws. NARAL still exists today as one of America's chief pro-abortion lobby groups. At one time, Nathanson was the director of the largest freestanding abortion facility in the world. One of the premier pro-abortion activists, Nathanson also worked with Betty Friedan to fight for the wholesale legalization of abortion in America. Their efforts were a huge factor in the Roe v. Wade case.[2]

Nathanson, who estimated that he was involved in approximately 75,000 abortions over the course of his career, even oversaw the abortion of his own child. (In the 1940s, Nathanson performed an abortion on his girlfriend.[3])

But something came into the world one day, changing Bernard Nathanson's life forever. That something was a new technology called ultrasound. Please allow me to take a step back here and hand the microphone to Dr. Nathanson. He can explain things a lot better than I can, so I'm going to let him take over for a moment. If you would please, Dr. Nathanson?

"A favorite pro-abortion tactic is to insist that the definition of when life begins is impossible, that the question is a theological or moral or philosophical one, anything but a scientific one.

"Foetology makes it undeniably evident that life begins at conception and requires all the protection and safeguards that any of us enjoy.

"Why, you may well ask, do some American doctors who are privy to the findings of foetology, discredit themselves by carrying out abortions? Simple arithmetic at $300.00 a time 1.55 million abortions (wording in context) means an industry generating $500,000,000 annually, of which most goes into the pocket of the physician doing the abortion.

"I am often asked what made me change my mind. How did I change from prominent abortionist to pro-life advocate? In 1973, I became director of obstetrics of a large hospital in New York City and had to set up a prenatal research unit, just at the start of a great new technology which we now use every day to study the foetus (sic) in the womb.

"It is clear that permissive abortion is purposeful destruction of what is undeniably human life. It is an impermissible act of deadly violence. One must concede that unplanned pregnancy is a wrenchingly difficult dilemma. But to look for its solution in a deliberate act of destruction is to trash the vast resourcefulness of human ingenuity, and to surrender the public weal to the classic utilitarian answer to social problems."[4]

The article I'm quoting here concludes Nathanson's statements thus: "In the early 70s Nathanson began to have doubts about abortion, and with the advent of ultrasound he persuaded a colleague who was doing 15-20 abortions a day to record an abortion using the new technology. After the two of them viewed the results his colleague never did another abortion, and Nathanson wrote, 'I...was shaken to the very roots of my soul by what I saw."[5]

In the end, Nathanson, who in his earlier years identified himself as a "Jewish atheist," converted to Roman Catholicism. The transformation from abortionist and standard-bearer for the pro-abortion cause to tireless warrior for the lives of the unborn was due almost entirely to his having seen the light of truth shone on the reality of his occupation. That light of truth was the technology known as ultrasound. As a fighter for life, Nathanson filmed two significant documentaries, including "Eclipse of Reason," which exposed the evil practice of late-term abortions. He also authored several tell-all books, one of which was an autobiography titled "The Hand of God: A Journey from Death to Life by the Abortion Doctor Who Changed His Mind."[6]

I could continue on, going much further and deeper into both science and the Bible. I'm going to leave off here, though, because if anyone out there has read this far and he remains steadfast in the belief that life begins at any point after conception, then no amount of facts will persuade him otherwise. Once a man's foolish heart has been darkened, and once he has been given over to a debased mind, this is a man who has been immunized against all truth. When he's reached this level, this is no longer a man who *won't* hear the truth; he'll be someone who tragically *can't* hear it.

31

MEANINGLESS OR MEANINGFUL?

Lamech didn't value the lives of his two brides any more than he did the young man he murdered. He kept his women around only because he could take what he wanted from them. His adversary, on the other hand, got in the way of whatever it was he wanted, so he killed him. It seems plausible to me that the man Lamech assassinated might have tried to say something about his adulterous lifestyle. Perhaps God had put Lamech's victim in his path to try and talk some sense into him.

Do you stop and ask these kinds of questions about yourself? Do you ever think about why God has put you in the paths of others? Or why He might have put other people into yours? Why do you suppose God went to the trouble of creating all those little ones that were put to death before they saw the light of day? Did God want those babies dead?

As you ponder these questions, remember our text for this section of the book. God has disconnected the mind of the man who deliberately pushed Him from his thoughts (as it says in Rom. 1:28, "...they did not like to retain God in their knowledge..."). When that happens, all the empty space up there in his head is promptly replaced with different thoughts. That's what is meant by Rom. 1:29, which goes on to explain that the unregenerate man moves quickly from hearing the truth about the Lord to rejecting Him, and this will cause God to allow him to be "filled with all unrighteousness."

The rest of v. 29 and vs. 30-31 help us understand what is meant by the term "all unrighteousness." As I noted previously, it is one thing to not know God; it's quite another to be introduced to Him and then willfully repudiate Him. When someone goes through life and is never confronted with the gospel of the Lord Jesus, that's a tragedy; that person will die and go to eternal perdition.

However, when a person is presented with the words of life but fails to respond in the singular acceptable way that God commands, that is a catastrophe that defies adequate description. Such a man will enter hell with both eyes open, and the suffering he must endure for all eternity will actually be worse than it will for the man who died in ignorance.

Come again? Did I just hear you ask, "What are the words of life?" Oh, my friend, I'm so thrilled you brought that up! Please, let me tell you. But before I do, I must give you a couple of disclaimers. First, the words you're about to read have behind them the force of everything to come for all eternity. Once you've read the next several paragraphs, you will be more accountable to the Lord God than you are at this moment. Please don't laugh. Don't giggle. Don't even smile. This is no joke. If you dare to continue reading, there will be no going back. Every man is fully responsible to God for the amount of "light," or divinely imparted information, to which he is exposed over the course of his life.

I know what some of you out there are thinking right now. You're saying to yourselves, "Well, if I'm answerable to God for what you tell me, then I'll just bypass the rest of this chapter. God can't hold me responsible for what I don't know!" Nice try, but it doesn't work that way. There's a second disclaimer I need for you to know: Ignorance is no excuse. Think back to the earliest parts of this book, and you'll recall what we saw in Rom. 1:20, which says that you have already been given plenty of knowledge about God. The mere awareness that you have of the world around you, the ground beneath you, and the sky above you is more than enough for God to condemn you. Without reading this book any further, without reading any book from here on out, without learning one solitary thing more than you now know, you have far more than enough knowledge for God to judge you fairly and judge you righteously. Trust me in this, you do not want God's justice. What you want is His mercy.

Since you know too much, you may as well go ahead and read on. Look at it this way: You have nothing to lose, and everything to gain. So take a deep breath, turn off the TV and the computer, and forge ahead. Are you ready? Here we go: "For God so loved the world that He gave His only begotten Son, that whoever believes in Him should not perish but have everlasting life" (John 3:16). I know almost no one who hasn't heard this verse, so chances are good that you haven't been exposed to anything new just yet. You might even be able to quote these words from memory.

But do you know the words that follow? John 3:17-18: "For God did not send His Son into the world to condemn the world, but that the world through Him might be saved. He who believes in Him is not condemned; but he who does not believe is condemned already, because he has not believed in the name of the only begotten Son of God." Friend, the gospel is "good news." That's what the word "gospel" in the Greek language means. But it is also a warning. The gospel, properly presented and correctly understood, is a message that's a two-edged sword. One edge says "welcome to eternal life," while the other pronounces everlasting judgment in a place the Bible calls the lake of fire.

An excellent summary of this bedrock doctrine is found at the end of John 3. It reads: "He who believes in the Son has everlasting life; and he who does not believe the Son shall not see life, but the wrath of God abides on him" (v. 36). The good news is that you don't have to work your way to heaven. The reason for this is because you <u>can't</u> earn a place in heaven. The Lord Jesus paid the full price of your redemption on the cross. One of the clearest and most repeated themes of the Bible is that all your good works have absolutely no power whatsoever to save you (cf. Isa. 64:6; Rom. 3:20; Gal. 2:16).

If you can't please God by anything you could do, then how can you be saved? John 5:24: "Most assuredly, I say to you, he who hears My word and believes in Him who sent Me has everlasting life, and shall not come into judgment, but has passed from death into life." If your salvation was written out like a recipe, it would read "100% God, 0% you." You could even write this little equation on a 3x5 card and keep it in your pocket as a reminder. If you want to be saved from your sins, if you want to avoid hell and gain heaven, there is but one way for that to occur. Believe on the Lord Jesus Christ, and you will be saved (cf. Acts 16:31).

That's the essence of the gospel. I don't want to leave it at that, though, because I need to flesh out something I've only briefly touched on. Now that you know that all of your eternal hope rests in Jesus and the perfect sacrifice He made when He died on the cross, you must take action. You must believe on Him and trust Him alone for your salvation. If you fail to take this all-important step, you will be punished forever in a place of everlasting torment and suffering. There's a catch, though. Now that you've been informed of the solitary way that you can be saved, and now that you've been warned of the consequences if you don't act upon it, your eternal punishment will actually be more severe than what it would have been had you not read this chapter.

Just as there are varying degrees of reward for those who inherit eternal life, there are contrariwise multiple levels of pain and sorrow that will fall on the unrepentant. Carefully read Luke 12:42-48, and pay extra close attention when you get to those last two verses. In v. 47, Jesus explains that the person who knew what God expected of him but disobeyed Him anyway will be punished severely. For the man who didn't know what God demanded, the Savior says (v. 48) that such a one will be judged but less harshly. However, hell is still hell, and to languish there forever will be more painful than any of us can grasp.

However, the more someone knows about what God has said, the more accountable that person is. The Australian Aborigine who died without having heard the Name of Jesus will die in his sin, and the weight of God's judgment upon him will be heavy. But the man who sat in a pew week after week and year after year, having heard God's Word explained to him over and over again, having never responded to that precious Word, may I say to you that such a man could only wish that his sentence were as light as that Aborigine's. It's what Jesus meant by what He said in Luke 12:48: to whom much is given, much shall be required.

Life is either meaning*less* or it's meaning*ful*. If the atheists are right, then your life is completely and utterly meaningless. If the atheists are right, then your death means the end of your existence. If the atheists are right, your life will end and then you will have an eternity of… nothing. If that's true, then it makes no difference what you do with your life. Just let your life be one long beer commercial. Live for yourself, grab all the gusto you can (whatever that's supposed to mean), and seek your personal pleasure and satisfaction at the expense of everything else. If there's no bliss in heaven, no misery in hell, then do as you like! If everything you do in this life accounts for nothing after you're gone, then what's the point of doing anything for anyone besides yourself?

If I may, I'd like to offer you an alternative to that sad and utterly hopeless worldview. I say to you, my friend, that your life does matter. It matters right now, and it will matter forever. Yes, your life matters to others. Yes, your life will matter to people who come after you. But your life matters, most of all, to you. What you do today has a ripple effect for eternity. The Bible says that you are not your own, that you were bought for a price (I Cor. 6:19-20; I Pet. 1:17-19). This truth is the key to understanding why you're here. You are here to glorify God (I Cor. 6:20), and the reward for your obedience will last forever and ever.

As we wrap up this next to last section of the book I want to make one last observation. If you go back to the first verse this book is tracking, which is Rom. 1:18, you will read that God's wrath is revealed through His judgment against ungodliness and unrighteousness. Lamech is a perfect example of how that judgment looks. He worshiped himself instead of God. He lived for himself instead of others. He was more interested in satisfying his prurient interests than he was in loving a wife. He murdered a man and then went so far as to announce that God would bless him for it. Lamech lived his life as though it were meaningless. Today, Lamech knows all too well how wrong he was. And to think, his slide into hell started when he made one mistake, the mistake of rejecting the truth about God.

By now, it should be abundantly clear to you that not only is America under the judgment of God, but also that we've been on the receiving end of His chastisement for a long time. To be candid, I've grown weary of hearing preachers and public figures warn us that "If we don't repent, God's going to judge us." I think that one of the scariest elements of God's discipline is the fact that so few people even recognize it when it's happening to them and all around them. I guess that must be part of the darkening of the foolish heart. A people under judgment become futile in their thinking, and they profess to be wise, although they became fools. They continue to look for answers, even salvation, in man and government instead of looking to the Lord. And where did it all begin? When they traded the truth of God in for a lie.

Now that we've established where we are on God's "judgment scale," there's but one subject left to explore: What do we as Christians do about it? I hope to answer this all-important question in the next section. If you're ready, turn the page. Let's find out what the Almighty expects from His people in these dark days.

PART FOUR

THE FINAL STRAW

"Who, knowing the righteous judgment of God, that those who practice such things are deserving of death, not only do the same but also approve of those who practice them" – Romans 1:32

32

A CALL TO ARMS

When America was still in its fledgling years, a French philosopher named Alexis de Tocqueville visited our land to learn how a ragtag band of settlers could defeat the likes of the British Empire. In his book "Death of a Nation," John Stormer wrote of de Tocqueville: "He looked for the greatness of America in her harbors and rivers, her fertile fields and boundless forests, mines and other natural resources. He studied America's schools, her Congress, and her matchless Constitution without comprehending America's power. Not until he went into the churches of America and heard pulpits 'aflame with righteousness' did he understand the secret of her genius and strength. De Tocqueville returned to France and wrote: 'America is great because America is good, and if America ever ceases to be good, America will cease to be great.'"[1]

Proverbs 14:34 says that "Righteousness exalts a nation, but sin is a reproach to any people." From this one short verse, I derive three vital truths. First, there is a difference between righteousness and sin. Second, God expects us to know and understand that difference. And third, the consequences of righteousness are different from the consequences of sin. I hate to be the one to apply pressure to the body of Christ, but if America is to have any hope of recovery, it will come first and foremost through the church.

I Peter 4:17 warns the people of God that His judgment falls on the house of God before it lands on anyone else. One of the key contributors to America's "Second Great Awakening" (a revival that blanketed much of the U.S. in the early to mid-1800s) was a man named Charles Finney. In regard to the principle given to us by the apostle Peter, Finney said this: "If there is a decay of conscience, the pulpit is responsible for it. If the public press lacks moral discernment, the pulpit is responsible for it. If the church is degenerate and worldly, the pulpit is responsible for it. If the world loses its interest in Christianity, the pulpit is responsible for it. If Satan rules in our halls of legislation, the pulpit is responsible for it. If our politics become so corrupt that the very foundations of our government are ready to fall away, the pulpit is responsible for it."[2]

Finney held to several doctrines that I am confident are in error. This, however, is not one of them. Pastors play a vital role in the lives of their congregants, and the things taught from the pulpit work their way into the hearts and minds of the people in the pews. One of the chief reasons America is finding herself in the pickle she's in is because of the silence of her pulpits in the face of an epidemic of gross national sin. The muzzling of our pastors has translated into a moral paralysis that is infecting entire congregations throughout the land.

Back to I Peter 4:17, the verse ends with a rhetorical question that should make us tremble. Peter says that if judgment begins with the body of Christ, "…what will be the end of those who do not obey the gospel of God?" Unsaved people have no capacity to behave in any other way than, well, unsaved (I'm referring again to I Corinthians 2:10-16.) That's why everyone who is not under the blood of the Savior continues to look for the answers to our problems in all the wrong places. Neither science, nor education, nor anything or anyone in all humanity made America the greatest nation in history. GOD made America great. Now that we're kicking Him out, our greatness has evaporated.

I'm getting ready to share something very important with you, so please pay close attention. Strive hard not to lash back against this truth, okay? Here goes. It makes very little difference who wins the next election, be it for president, congress, city council, or labor commissioner. God will never, no never honor a wicked society with righteous leaders, or at the very least He will keep righteous leaders from having any worthwhile impact on their colleagues or constituents. Do not forget this: Godly leaders are the result, not the cause, of a godly society. If God is what made America great, then the removal of God is what is leading America to her demise.

The world will keep trying and keep trying and keep trying to find the answers in man, in science, in education, in "saving the planet," or in any of a host of other wrong places. The one place they will never look is the one place true peace and hope can be found, and that, of course, is in the Lord Jesus Christ, the Mighty God. If you are a Christian, it is your task to "walk worthy of your calling" (Eph. 4:1-3; Col. 1:9-11; I Thess. 2:10-12). The lion's share of this book's remaining pages will be devoted to giving you tips and suggestions on how to do just that. It will be much easier for you if your pastor and your church will travel this road with you, but you may have to prepare to take the journey with no one at your side but the Lord Himself. Either way, you're going to need to be properly equipped.

33

WHAT LITTLE I CAN DO, I WILL DO

On November 13, 2014, U.S. Speaker of the House John Boehner stood behind the lectern on the U.S. House floor and introduced Hamad Chebli to the entire body of the U.S. House of Representatives. Chebli, who is the Imam for the Islamic Center of Central Jersey, stood up and took his place behind the podium after his introduction by Speaker Boehner. Chebli then went on to pray for more than three minutes, invoking the name if his god Allah and asking for his blessing on the proceedings of the nation's business. Throughout the prayer, the congressmen bowed in humility and reverence to this nonexistent deity.[1]

A little more than 15 months prior to that, the same Speaker Boehner in the same House chamber introduced a Washington, D.C. Imam, Talib Shareef, who then stood behind the same lectern and offered the same kind of prayer, again to the same mythological god.[2]

As bizarre as these events are, the surreal nature of it all is magnified by the fact that evidence of America's Christian heritage is indelibly chiseled into dozens of buildings and monuments scattered across the District of Columbia. For instance, our nation's motto, "In God We Trust," is prominently displayed in the chambers of both the U.S. House and Senate. In the Capitol Rotunda, there are artistic renderings of things like a prayer service with Christopher Columbus, the baptism of Pocahontas, and pilgrims participating in acts of Christian worship.

The Ten Commandments can be found in multiple highly visible areas, such as the National Archives, the Library of Congress, and in numerous locations at the U.S. Supreme Court, including a frieze above the seating for the Justices. The Washington Monument, the Jefferson Memorial, and Lincoln Memorial are replete with Scripture quotes and references. In the Library of Congress, there is a permanent exhibit of both the Giant Bible of Mainz and the Gutenberg Bible. Etched into the walls of the library are verses like John 1:5, Proverbs 4:7, Micah 6:8; and Psalm 19:1.[3]

Let me be very clear on a few major points. Allah is not God. Muslims are not Christians. America was founded on Christianity by Christian people. These are facts, and they are not in dispute. I know of no quotes from the Qur'an (or any other Muslim writings, for that matter) to have ever been stamped or carved into any historically significant American edifice. America is not a Muslim nation any more than it is a Hindu nation or a Buddhist nation or Zoroastrian nation. America is in spiritual decline, to put it mildly. But there is no argument about the fact that America was founded on the Bible and the principles that can be found exclusively in that Book.

Lamech invoked the wrong God. It's not that he didn't know who God was, because he knew something of what God graciously did for Cain. What Lamech failed to understand was why God promised that He would protect Cain. It's not enough to know who God is; one must have a relationship with Him. Similarly, Muslims worship and serve a god that is not the God of the Bible. The result of this is that they do not and cannot have a right relationship with Him; the key doctrines of Islam preclude any possibility that a practicing Muslim could be in right standing before the Throne.

Why, then, do we have American leaders in the American Capitol conducting America's political business on behalf of their American constituents by having two different men on two separate occasions to call upon a god that has no connection to American history? That's the question I posed to one of my U.S. senators, who was a member of the U.S. House of Representatives when both of these incidents occurred. Please keep your finger here, and turn to page 232. There you will find Appendix A, which contains three documents. The first is a copy of the letter I sent to my senator about these two incidents. The second document is a written reply I received, not from the senator I contacted, but from my congressman. The last article is a letter I sent to the senator in response to the congressman's correspondence to me. Please read these three letters, then come back and pick up here.

This round-robin sort of communication made for a weird interaction between me and my representatives. Since I never heard back from my senator after my second missive to him, I ended up with no real answer. To my mind, these terribly unfortunate events remain unresolved.

The same kind of scenario occurred when I made my voice heard after the June 26, 2015 Supreme Court debacle over what constitutes marriage. I tried to reach all five of my state's congressmen and both of our senators. The letter I sent to these seven representatives bore no fruit, so I wrote to the entire U.S. House Judiciary Committee. Please press "pause" here, turn to Appendix B on page 239, and read the letter there. (That letter has yet to receive a reply as well.) I'll meet you back here when you're finished.

These things are sure to sound "intolerant" to the 21st century ear, but that's because 21st century Americans are being taught that all roads lead to the same God. For all those who subscribe to this notion, and for all those who believe that Christianity is "too narrow" in its doctrines, and for all those who have a "Coexist" bumper sticker on their car, I would suggest they try their beliefs out on a practicing Muslim. If he's worth anything as a follower of Mohammad's teachings, he will tell you in no uncertain terms that your worldview is wrong. It turns out that everyone is narrow in their thinking, even those who have the softheaded idea that everyone is right. No matter what you believe, you are sure to offend or exclude someone. What matters, then, is who and what you believe, not how discourteous your faith appears to others.

I'm not trying to defame anyone here, nor is it my desire to toot my own horn. I have a solitary objective, and it involves you. I see citizenship as a duty that requires far more than just going to the voting booth once every few years. Thomas Jefferson is credited with having said that "eternal vigilance is the price of liberty." By sharing a little of my behind-the-scenes work with you, it is my prayer that you would take up your pen and write. Maybe you already do that. If so, many thanks, and keep up the good work! But if the thought of contacting your representatives is new to you, please let me encourage you to get involved with your government. I don't know when being patriotic turned into a sinful act for the church, but we need to get over that. Government is God's idea, and He expects us to participate in it.

Nobody likes politics less than I do. And, just as a little aside, I have a decent handle on where we are on God's prophetic timetable. (If you've read my first book, you know whereof I speak.) It was a long time ago that I lost count of how many elected officials, from city councilman to the man in the White House and nearly everybody in between, that I've written, e-mailed, called, or petitioned.

As I look back, I ask myself, "Honestly, how much good has all this work done?" Answer: Not much, but probably more than I realize. God does not command me to be successful; He commands me to be obedient. The results are up to Him. May I say to you that the very same is true of you? That's why I try to live by the Ted Merritt creed: "I am just one man, so I can't do much. But what little I can do, I will do."

And so must you.

34

HOW BADLY DO YOU WANT IN?

"I know your works, that you are neither cold nor hot. I could wish you were cold or hot. So then, because you are lukewarm, and neither cold nor hot, I will vomit you out of My mouth" (Rev. 3:15-16). These terrible words, uttered by none other than the Lord of Glory, were directed at a first century church in Laodicea. In Revelation 2-3, Jesus dictated to the apostle John a total of seven letters, one to each of seven churches. The church at Laodicea was the only one of the bunch that received no praise. As you see by the strong words that Christ has for this church, they'd be better off if they hated Him! If there's one thing our God can't stand, it is indifference. He actually prefers antipathy to apathy.

I can understand why God would be more displeased with an indifferent disciple than with a zealous enemy. As I noted earlier, atheists talk more about God than just about anybody else does, but your run-of-the-mill Sunday morning Christian will show up at church and warm the same pew like a bump on a log. He never changes, never grows, and never makes an effort to share his faith with anyone. The atheist's day hasn't been worth living until he's made at least one defamatory comment against his Maker. But just by saying something – even if it's bad –

about God, this in itself will force others around him to have their thoughts directed toward eternal matters in some form or fashion. The nominal Christian, on the other hand, seldom says anything to anyone about a Supreme Being or the hereafter. He thinks he's done more than enough for God by showing up to church every few months. Jesus responds, "Give Me the guy who hates Me; I prefer him."

There's almost no one more useless to God than a lazy Christian. By now, you can probably see that Lamech would have fallen into that category. We all know the type. It's the guy who's not afraid to carelessly toss God's name into a conversation once in a blue moon. He's blind to the fact that every time he opens his yap to mention something about God or Jesus, he's only showing his ignorance about who God is or what we know about the mind of Christ (I Cor. 2:16 again). I can't say it enough times: God doesn't want you to know about Him; He wants you to know Him.

Let me give you a rather graphic illustration from a while back that may help me get this point across. On December 3, 1979, the British rock group The Who performed at Riverfront Coliseum in Cincinnati before a sellout crowd of more than 18,000 adoring fans. The majority of tickets were general admission, so seating for most of the attendees was first-come, first-served. Not long before the show was scheduled to begin, tragedy struck. I'll let Wikipedia pick up the story from here:

> "A few hours before the show, a sizeable crowd had already gathered at the front of the arena. Entry to the arena was through a series of individual doors all along the front of the arena, as well as a few doors at each side. The crowd focused at each of the doors. The doors were not opened at the scheduled time, causing the crowd to become increasingly agitated and impatient. During this period, The Who undertook a late sound check. Some members of the crowd heard this and mistakenly believed that the concert was starting. Some people in the back of the crowd began pushing toward the front, but this rush soon dissipated as the crowd realized that no doors had been opened and the concert would not yet have begun.
>
> "A pair of doors was finally opened at the far right of the main entrance. As concertgoers streamed in through those two doors, those waiting in front of all of the other doors began pushing forward. After a short period of waiting and then knocking on the doors and the glass next to the doors, the crowd realized that none of the many remaining doors would be opened. The entire crowd began surging and pushing toward the sole two doors which had been opened. This caused many people to get trampled while some suffered more serious injuries. Eleven concertgoers were unable to escape the throng of people pushing toward them and were killed by asphyxiation. There were a total of twenty-six other injuries."[1]

Every time I read Luke 16:16, I think of that horrible event. Here's what Jesus said: "The law and the prophets were until John. Since that time the kingdom of God has been preached, and everyone is pressing into it." The word "pressing" in this verse is the Greek word "biazo," which means "to force, i.e. (reflexively) to crowd oneself (into), or (passively) to be seized: -- press, suffer violence." Jesus was telling the Pharisees (His audience there in Luke 16) that those who enter into God's kingdom do it with total abandon.

I remember the day I got saved. I was at work, and I was out making deliveries in the company truck. I had started listening to Christian talk radio a few months earlier. (Only God knows how that new routine entered my daily life.) Anyway, it was Good Friday – March 28, 1997 – and David Jeremiah was delivering a sermon about the Crucifixion. I sat in a customer's parking lot at 9:00 o'clock in the morning, riveted to my radio, unable to get out of the cab of that truck until Pastor Jeremiah finished. He gave an invitation at the close of his sermon, and I don't think I'll ever forget the things that were racing through my mind at that moment. I didn't fully understand who Jesus was, and I barely grasped what He went through for me, but I knew I was a wretched sinner and on my way to hell. I knew that if I didn't grab on to Jesus' outstretched hand at that very moment that I might forever be lost. In that instant, there was no army, no government, no pack of rabid wolverines that could have kept me from my Savior.

Debbie and I have a friend who came to the cross on April 18, 2013. His name is Chuck. We had been friends with Chuck since 1997, right around the time that Debbie and I were both saved. We witnessed to him, prayed for him, counseled and advised him. But nothing really changed in Chuck's life until the day he said yes to Jesus (which was April 18, 2013). I had the privilege of baptizing him. At his baptism, Chuck read aloud a letter that he'd sent to a friend of his who couldn't understand the drastic change in him. I asked him if I could share this wonderful letter with you, and he said yes. It is a marvelous testimony of who God is and what it is He does when He brings a lost sinner to salvation. Here is that letter:

"My Dear Friend,

I owe you an apology for the other day, and as a friend I feel that I owe you an explanation as to why. I have struggled for many years about who I am and what I've become. My gambling was way out of control, along with drinking and a lot of built-up anger, hatred and just a dislike for my own self. I came to know over the years of what the Bible says and how with God's grace you can truly have internal peace and bring change to your life through salvation. A few weeks ago I hit rock bottom, finally came to realize I can't do this on my own, and I asked Jesus to become my Lord and Savior and was born again.

The old Chuck is dead and, with the Lord's grace and help, so too are the gambling, the drinking, and my old way of life. You are an old friend of mine and a very sweet person who will always hold a special part of my heart. However, the bars, the drinking, and the gambling all need to remain in the past, for I need to build my strength through Jesus Christ for my future. I will not be a hypocrite and say one thing and live the other; the world is way too full of people calling themselves Christians and misleading all that is around them, and I won't be that way.

I still consider you a good friend and I hope you feel the same way, and it's not to say we can't have lunch or dinner, or perhaps take in a movie or a play sometime, and of course you're always welcome to join me in church. I'm still the same goofy Chuck or 'dork' as you like to say, except I am no longer lost, for I have finally found Christ."

As for Luke 16:16, I believe that Jesus was telling the Pharisees that this is how He saves His elect. The child of God, once he's passed from death to life (John 5:24), can't be kept from his Lord. Yes, we all stumble. We all sin. Even after we've been saved, we go astray. We do it regularly, often, and sometimes even for extended periods. However, God has an unbreakable grip on every last one that belongs to Him, and not a single one will ever be lost (John 10:27-29).

A crowd of people, desperate to get into an arena, clambered over one another and fought and scratched and even killed so they could spend a few measly hours enthralled by an earthly pleasure. Jesus has thrust open the door to eternal life. How much more should His little ones latch onto Him, letting neither anyone nor anything stand in their way of getting to where He is (cf. Luke 12:1)! Adrian Rogers used to say that faith is believing God in spite of appearances, and it is obeying God in spite of consequences. May God grant each of us that kind of faith.

35

LENGTHENING SHADOWS

At the beginning of this fourth and final portion of the book, I said that I wanted to give you some pointers on how to live as a Christian ought during this hour of trial. As Americans, we haven't been accustomed to living under the intense heat of God's refining fire. One of the primary themes of this work, though, is to show you that we are now truly experiencing a bona fide sample of heaven's chastisement. I wouldn't go so far as to say that we have God's undivided attention, for God is well able to keep up everything that's happening in the entire universe, and He does this constantly and perpetually.

I am saying, however, that God is now handling America very differently from how He used to treat her. And because He is executing His wrath upon us, there are some things I wish to impart to you as a sort of survival guide. I intentionally chose not to give you an itemized to-do list, because I, like most Americans, am navigating through some previously uncharted territory. I've lived my whole life as a spoiled brat, enjoying the blessings of God without so much as a "Thank You" to Him for His magnanimous grace. I've never once known, not even for a minute, what it is like to be hungry. I've never been homeless. I've never been without a single need for one second of my life. What's more, I don't know anyone who has.

It appears that humanity in general has a hard time with God's blessings. After living with them for a little while, we start treating the Lord like He's our own personal genie. But, as Debbie likes to say, God is NOT Santa Claus. We tend to get more impatient and increasingly demanding of a good God who – please hear me – owes us nothing. God does not owe us food, clothing, or shelter. He most assuredly does not owe us entertainment and happiness, nor does He owe us the means to acquire such things. Yet the more God has given us, the more we've been willing to take. The more we've taken, the more we've come to expect from Him. We've become a difficult and ungrateful people, and God does not take kindly to those who don't properly appreciate His hospitality.

The longer I've worked on this book, the more convicted I've become about the blessings of God and how poorly I've responded to them. I'm not giving you a grocery list of things to say, think, do or act out in America's time of judgment because I have no personal experience of it beyond what any other American has had up to now. My goal here is to share with you what I can from the Scriptures and hopefully prompt your thinking, so that you may also be open to hearing what God would have you to do as we continue to anxiously wait for the Rapture of the body of Christ.

Far too many Christians have misplaced faith. They believe on the Lord Jesus as their Savior, but they still want to stick around for awhile so they can watch their grandkids grow up. They sometimes even say that they know Jesus is coming back someday, but not now. My response to that is in the form of a question: Why not now? We know for a fact that Jesus is returning to this earth one day to set up His kingdom here. (That's even in the first half of the Lord's Prayer.) Jesus also said that we don't know the day or the hour of His return, but we do know the signs to look for (which are all around us now!).

If Jesus could come and take us home in the Rapture at any moment (and He can – see James 5:8-9), then what's keeping that day from being today? If there's nothing preventing the Rapture from being today (and there is nothing), then it stands to reason that we should be all the more committed to doing His work (cf. Luke 19:11-13).

Being about our Father's business includes our unflinching steadfastness in standing up for His righteousness (Matt. 6:33). Proverbs 17:15 says: "He who justifies the wicked, and he who condemns the just, both of them alike are an abomination to the Lord." I don't remember where I heard this, so I can't give proper credit to whoever said it. Obviously, this fact doesn't diminish its truth, so I'm going to repeat it here.

The descent of a godly society toward a sinful one occurs in three stages. In the first stage, the people take an activity that used to be condemned as evil and they begin to celebrate it. This leads to the second stage, which is when the society takes an activity that was once celebrated and they collectively condemn it. After that comes the final stage, and that is a frontal assault on the principle of Proverbs 17:15. Here we see the society turning against the people who refuse to celebrate the previously condemned activity. In other words, it's not good enough for a man to remain silent when asked to give his thoughts on a reprehensible or perverse action. He must now voice his hearty approval of the wickedness, no matter how loathsome.

This is exactly what is meant by Rom. 1:32, where it says "...that those who practice such things are deserving of death, not only do the same but <u>also approve of those who practice them</u>" (emphasis mine). Lamech murdered a young man, but his wives didn't admonish him, nor did society punish him. We need to remember that our silence in the face of evil is the exact same thing as our acceptance of it.

Here in our country, God's plan for marriage was systematically thrown over and replaced with a flagitious one. From there, it took very little time for Satan's troops to mobilize against those who'd dare to try and oppose such atrocities.

You and I are going to find ourselves in an ever-shrinking minority. We must stand firm, though, because God will save all who endure to the end (Matt. 10:22; Mark 13:13). The world is not going to get better on its own. In fact, it will only get worse from here on out (II Tim. 3:12-13). Not until the Lord comes with all His saints to set up the Kingdom will the world be as God intended (Rev. 19:11-20:6). Until then, the ride is going to get progressively rougher.

36

A GODLY HATRED

You know how little kids just blurt out things that their elders don't have the guts to say? "Gee, Aunt Erma, you're really fat!" "Mom, this casserole tastes yucky!" "I don't wanna play with Billy. He smells funny!" You know, stuff like that.

When I was that age, I was never afraid to say that I "hated" someone. After years of being corrected by my parents and my Sunday school teachers, I finally learned that it's impolite to say that you "hate" a person. I ultimately gave in to societal pressure and started going with the less offensive "I don't like so-and-so." But can I tell you a little secret? To this day, I still don't really know the difference between "dislike" of someone and "hating" them.

Well, that's not completely true. Now that I've done the research for this portion of the book, I do have a little better idea of the difference. But it still ain't much of one.

Anyway, the subject of hatred has become an important one for me as I've prepared this volume. There were many times during my research and writing that I found myself boiling up with anger and, yes, what I would call hatred. As I considered my emotional state and the ramifications of my feelings, I realized that I needed to know if my reactions toward the people and situations would be what God wanted of me.

I'm now going to pose this question to you. Is it possible to hate someone and still love God? This may not be hard for you to answer, but I've wrestled with the matter for some months now. Because I believe it's vital for us to understand hatred and the role it should (or shouldn't) play in the life of the Christian, I sense the need to devote some space to it. I might also point out the fact that the unsaved world does not understand what true biblical love is (as we saw earlier in the book), so it's easy to see how that same world would likewise have an unbiblical view of hatred.

In Psalm 139:19-22, David expounded upon his hatred for the wicked. He wrote: "Oh, that You would slay the wicked, O God! Depart from me, therefore, you bloodthirsty men. For they speak against You wickedly; Your enemies take Your name in vain. Do I not hate them, O Lord, who hate You? And do I not loathe those who rise up against You? I hate them with perfect hatred; I count them my enemies." If you read Psalm 31:6, you'll see very similar musings from this mighty man of God.

In II Chronicles 18, King Ahab of Israel and King Jehoshaphat of Judah made an alliance to join in battle against Syria. After wicked Ahab died, the righteous king Jehoshaphat was visited by a prophet. II Chr. 19:1-2 says this: "Then Jehoshaphat the king of Judah returned safely to his house in Jerusalem. And Jehu the son of Hanani the seer went out to meet him, and said to King Jehoshaphat, 'Should you help the wicked and love those who hate the Lord? Therefore the wrath of the Lord is upon you." The short version of this story is that God was angry with His servant Jehoshaphat because he had made friends with an enemy of the Lord.

God even gives us examples of people whom He hates. One such person is the man Esau: "The burden of the word of the Lord to Israel by Malachi. 'I have loved you,' says the Lord. 'Yet you say, 'In what way have You loved us?' Was not Esau Jacob's brother?' Says the Lord. Yet Jacob I have loved; But Esau I have hated, and laid waste his mountains and his heritage for the jackals of the wilderness'" (Mal. 1:1-3). It's been said by many a Bible scholar that what God is saying here is that He loved Esau, He just loved him less than He loved Jacob. But is that what the word "hate" means here?

Turn toward the very front of your Bible, and read Gen. 37:1-8. Three times in this passage it says that Joseph's brothers "hated" him (vs. 4, 5, 8). The word "hate" here in the Hebrew is "sah'nee," and it means "to hate personally: – enemy, foe, (be) hate(-ful), odious, utterly hate." Now go back to Malachi 1 read again vs. 2-3. The word "hated" here is the exact same word that was used three times in reference to Joseph's brothers and their feelings toward him. No matter what else can be said about these verses of Scripture, God clearly has different emotions toward Jacob than He does for Esau. The text, however, is plain: God hated Esau.

These verses are quoted in the New Testament as well. Please go to Romans 9, and when you get there, read vs. 8-13. That last word there in v. 13, the word "hated," is the Greek word "miseo." Strong's concordance defines the word this way: "to detest (esp. to persecute); by extension, to love less: – hate (-ful)." It's true that this word could potentially be used to mean that God merely "loved Esau less than He loved Jacob," but I don't buy that interpretation for two reasons: (1) This is a direct quote from an Old Testament passage, and the Hebrew word used there does not allow for the definition "loved less." It only means "hated;" and (2) Read v. 8 again. This verse is the key to understanding the whole passage. First comes the flesh, and then comes the spiritual.

Ishmael, the firstborn, represented the flesh (someone who clung to the things of this world), while Isaac, the younger son, symbolized the spirit (as in a man who had an authentic relationship with God). Esau, the elder, was the worldly man. His younger brother Jacob was the spiritual man. God did the calling, God did the deciding (v. 11), and God chose Jacob (see vs. 6-7). You can say that God "loved Esau less," but the fact remains that He chose Jacob over Esau, end of story. If you want to research why

God hated Esau but not Jacob, you probably don't have to look any further than the fact that Esau cared so little about what God was prepared to give him for an everlasting legacy that he traded it in for one lousy bowl of soup.

Now go to the other end of your Bible, and read Rev. 2:1-6, 12-16. Jesus was pleased with the church at Ephesus because they "hated" the false teachings of a group known as the Nicolaitans. The church in Pergamum, however, was scolded for their having embraced this group's erroneous beliefs. Hence, we know from these several examples that God reserves the right to "hate" both people and doctrines.

To at least some superficial degree, it would seem that the body of Christ has been given a license to do the same. Romans 12:9 says: "Let love be without hypocrisy. Abhor what is evil. Cling to what is good." "Apostygeo" is the Greek word for "abhor" here, and it means "to detest utterly: – abhor. To dislike, abhor, have a horror of." Now, for good measure, toss in a few more OT verses. Read the following: Psalm 34:14-16; 45:1-7; 97:10; 101:3; 119:104, 163; Prov. 8:13; Amos 5:14-15. There's no two ways about it, folks. We are commanded to hate evil!

The burning question now facing us is how we are to employ such hatred in our own lives. What does this hatred look like, and how far should it extend? I wish it were this simple, that what we see in these examples gives us a license to hate those who hate God or those who hate the brethren. The problem with that, though, is the fact that the New Testament teaches us something quite different. Please don't stop here, because, as Paul Harvey used to say, you need to hear "the rest of the story."

37

A GODLY LOVE

One of the most frequent accusations I hear from nonbelievers is that the Bible is "full of contradictions." My response is always the same: "Show me one, and let's work through it together." So far, I've had no takers.

What the Bible *is* full of is paradoxes. There is law versus grace, faith as opposed to works, dying to self that you might find life, giving in order to be blessed, and, well, for fear that I go off on a tangent, there are really too many to mention. A great example of a biblical paradox is found in Prov. 26:4-5, which gives a strange set of instructions. It reads: "Do not answer a fool according to his folly, Lest you also be like him. Answer a fool according to his folly, Lest he be wise in his own eyes." Now, I'm not going to address this particular conundrum, not because I'm chicken (as I really do know how to resolve this little brainteaser), but because I want stay on point and tackle the problem at hand.

Ecclesiastes 3:1-8 gives a fairly lengthy list of subjects that guide our thinking into some of these difficult areas. Said list ends with the observation that there is a time to love, a time to hate, a time of war, and a time of peace. Right there, we have all the proof we need that there are occasions that call for the child of God to "hate." This isn't really any great revelation. The trouble lies in the fact that the Bible doesn't always mark out clear parameters for when, what, and/or whom we should direct such hatred. To make matters worse, I still haven't been able to get a clear understanding of what hatred should look like.

Go back into the Scriptures, and find Gal. 5:16-24. Read these verses, paying particular attention to the word "hatred" there in v. 20. (It's the third word in the NKJV and NIV, translated in the NASB and ESV as "enmities" and "enmity," respectively.) This is a different Greek word here, "echthra," but it has a very similar meaning to the word "miseo" used in Romans. It means "hostility; by implication, a reason for opposition: – enmity, hatred." So here, hatred for our fellow man poses a serious problem, because v. 21 warns us that those who are engulfed by the things in the list preceding it (which includes hatred) "will not inherit the kingdom of God." This phrase is used several times by Paul as a metaphor stating that people guilty of practicing these types of sins will be sent to hell (cf. I Cor. 6:9-10; 15:50; Eph. 5:5). (I do want to interrupt myself here and point out the fact that people never go to hell for having committed a certain type of sin. There is no such thing as a "cardinal sin" or a type of sin that is unforgivable. People only go to hell for having rejected the way of salvation through God the Son. The sins listed in the above passages are reflective of the kinds of transgressions that an unsaved person would repeatedly commit. Or, to look at it from a different angle, saved individuals would not have a lifestyle that includes the regular commission of such sins.)

This line of thinking is perfectly consistent with the exhortation of Jesus in His sermon on the mount, where He utters these words: "You have heard that it was said, 'You shall love your neighbor and hate your enemy.' But I say to you, love your enemies, bless those who curse you, do good to those who hate you, and pray for those who spitefully use you and persecute you, that you may be sons of your Father in heaven; for He makes His sun rise on the evil and on the good, and sends rain on the just and on the unjust. For if you love those who love you, what reward have you? Do not even the tax collectors do the same? And if you greet your brethren only, what do you do more than others? Do not even the tax collectors do so? Therefore you shall be perfect, just as your Father in heaven is perfect" (Matt. 5:43-48).

Believe it or not, we're about to get a little relief from this dilemma. The ESV Study Bible gives us some good insights here, so I'm going to lean on their notes for a minute. Here's what they say in regard to vs. 43-44: "The OT never says that anyone should hate his enemy. This shows that, in His 'you have heard' statements (vs. 21, 27, 33, 38, 43), Jesus is correcting not the OT itself but only misinterpretations of the OT. God's hatred of evil was a central theme in the OT (e.g., Psa. 5:4-5). Consequently, those who embodied evil were understood to be God's enemies, and it was natural to hate them (cf. Ps. 26:4-5; 139:21-22), but such hatred is never commanded by God. (Verse 44 now): God hates evil, but He still brings many blessings in this life even to his enemies (v. 45) by means of 'common grace' (the favor that He gives to all people and not just believers). These blessings are intended to lead unbelievers to repentance (Acts 14:17; Rom. 2:4). Of course there is a sense in which God hates those who are resolutely and impenitently wicked (cf. Ps. 5:5; 11:5; Eph. 2:3), but God's blessings of common grace constitute His primary providential action toward mankind here and now."[1]

Along the same lines as Matthew 5 is Matt. 22:34-40. Read this passage, and while you're reading focus on the words "love your neighbor as yourself." Much of Jesus' teaching throughout His earthly ministry is an elucidation of what was given to the children of Israel in the Old Testament; that is exactly what He's done here. Read now Lev. 19:17-18 and you'll see what I mean. Those very same words, "love your neighbor as yourself," are found there in Leviticus. And just how do we show love to our neighbor? According to Leviticus, you put into action the following: (1) You do not hate your brother in your heart; (2) You rebuke your neighbor when he is in sin, and in this way you will not be called into account for his error; (3) You refuse to take vengeance against your neighbor when he has wronged you; and (4) You are not to bear a grudge against him.

There is a prescription for how the church is to implement discipline against a wayward member, and it is a simple formula. Still in Matthew, Jesus gives us His comprehensive plan for restoring a fallen brother: "Moreover if your brother sins against you, go and tell him his fault between you and him alone. If he hears you, you have gained your brother. But if he will not hear, take with you one or two more, that 'by the mouth of two or three witnesses every word may be established.' And if he refuses to hear them, tell it to the church. But if he refuses even to hear the church, let him be to you like a heathen and a tax collector" (Matt. 18:15-17).

This seems like a harsh practice, so much so that most churches these days decline to follow it. However, this is God's plan for "loving the brethren," both for those who are in sin as well as for protecting others from being adversely affected by the sinning brother. Also of note in regard to the subject of church discipline are passages like Rom. 16:17; I Cor. 5:9-13; Gal. 6:1. Read these verses, and it should become clearer that much of the problem surrounding "love" and "hate" for one another is that much of the body of Christ has lost a proper understanding for what these words really mean.

We're still not quite done, because now we have to take these two sides of the same coin and see how they work in harmony with one another. As you go through this next chapter, remember that our enemy is never our fellow man; it is the devil and his demons (Eph. 6:12).

38

SINGING WHILE THEY SCREAM

Dietrich Bonhoeffer was a German pastor who, late in World War II, acted in concert with a German resistance movement that had plotted an attempt on the life of the notorious Fuehrer Adolf Hitler. Bonhoeffer was tried in a Nazi concentration camp for his participation in the assassination plan. He was convicted, and on April 9, 1945, he was hanged by the Nazi government.[1]

Fast-forward now about 65 years, to Wichita, Kansas. On May 31, 2009, one George Richard Tiller was shot and murdered while passing out bulletins to congregants at the Reformation Lutheran Church, where he was a member and usher. Tiller had become a household name in some circles because of his lengthy and checkered career as an abortionist. He had gained such an unsavory reputation that he earned the nickname "Tiller the Killer," thanks to his repertoire of barbaric practices, which included the frequent performance of late-term abortions. Tiller was an unapologetic supporter of abortion in every form and at all stages of pregnancy, so he became a regular target of violence by people who claimed to be pro-life.[2]

Both Bonhoeffer and Tiller were victims of murder, but the similarities between these two men end there. Bonhoeffer was a Christian pastor who was motivated to kill Hitler, not because of his hatred for the despicable tyrant but because of his commitment to the preservation of human life. Tiller, on the other hand, was on the cutting edge (pun intended) of a profession bent on the destruction of human life. To make matters even worse, his church apparently had no trouble with his chosen vocation.

In the years leading up to his ascension to the throne, David had multiple opportunities to take down King Saul, who ultimately had become an enemy of God, of the nation of Israel, and even of David himself. Yet David never wavered in his devotion to Saul, and he did everything he could to protect him. This godly example set by David and honored by God gives me pause when I reflect on the actions of Bonhoeffer. To be frank, I struggle with whether or not he did right by participating in an assassination plot.

I am not a pacifist. I believe in the principles set forth in the "just war" doctrine. I am an advocate of the death penalty. The Bible is clear in each of these matters, and my worldview is reflective of that clarity. Hitler was one of the most evil leaders in history, and he needed to be put to death for his many crimes against humanity. But I don't know that his execution was a job for a civilian.

That said, I do not struggle with the events surrounding George Tiller. The person who killed him was a murderer. Even though Tiller himself was a professional mass murderer, he deserved a trial. Like Hitler, Tiller needed to be executed for his atrocities, but that was not the place of the man who assassinated him to step in and take the law into his own hands.

But the rub here is not about how Bonhoeffer and Tiller met their demise. It's about the church and the role it played in these two men's lives. Throughout the Holocaust, the body of Christ in Germany remained tragically silent, and they failed to intercede on behalf of those who were persecuted, even those who were chased all the way into the gas chambers. I have heard stories about the Jews who were rounded up by the Third Reich and were herded by train to various concentration camps, where they would be gassed and their bodies dumped into massive open trenches.

The trains that carried the condemned, crammed by the thousands into filthy boxcars, rumbled many miles through the countryside, and the air was filled with the moans and cries of the malnourished, broken victims. The story goes that on Sunday mornings, as these trains clickety-clacked into towns and cities along the way, the churches would always have their congregants engage in loud corporate song. As the trains approached each church, the worshipers belted out the hymns with increasing volume so they would drown out the bloodcurdling shrieks of the hapless enemies of the Fuehrer.

Was George Tiller's church any better? Let's all be honest with ourselves for a minute. The mountain of evidence put out against Planned Parenthood by the Center for Medical Progress was shocking to many, but was it really all that surprising? About the only thing those videos did was confirm what we should have known all along, that abortion is one of the ugliest crimes ever committed by a supposedly civilized society.

It's easy for me to sit here in my office, pecking away on my keyboard, and start thinking in my own self-righteous way that Tiller's church was guilty of a hideous crime. And make no mistake, they were guilty. They knew what he was doing, but they took no action to try and correct him. But if I look in the mirror, I have to ask if I've been any more righteous than Tiller's church. I've always known what the abortion industry was all about, but I have done so little to try and stop the screams of the babies in those awful clinics. Maybe we've all developed a habit of singing louder when the trains roll slowly by.

What did Lamech care about? Himself. What do people who refuse to worship God care about? Themselves. What do those who practice hedonism care about? Themselves. What do those who care nothing of the screaming Jews or the screaming babies ripped from their mothers' wombs care about? Themselves. This is the consummate picture of hatred. God has much to be angry about, and His people have many things over which we must repent.

39

SOLVING THE RIDDLE

To start this chapter, I'm going to give you a smattering of quotes from the New Testament epistles. I'll start with a couple of admonitions from the apostle Paul: "Repay no one evil for evil. Have regard for good things in the sight of all men. If it is possible, as much as depends on you, live peaceably with all men. Beloved, do not avenge yourselves, but rather give place to wrath; for it is written, 'Vengeance is Mine, I will repay,' says the Lord. Therefore 'If your enemy is hungry, feed him; If he is thirsty, give him a drink; For in so doing you will heap coals of fire on his head'" (Rom. 12:17-21).

"We are fools for Christ's sake, but you are wise in Christ! We are weak, but you are strong! You are distinguished, but we are dishonored! To the present hour we both hunger and thirst, and we are poorly clothed, and beaten, and homeless. And we labor, working with our own hands. Being reviled, we bless; being persecuted, we endure; being defamed, we entreat. We have been made as the filth of the world, the offscouring of all things until now" (I Cor. 4:10-13).

Now for some insights from Peter: "For to this you were called, because Christ also suffered for us, leaving us an example, that you should follow His steps: 'Who committed no sin, Nor was deceit found in His mouth'; who, when He was reviled, did not revile in return; when He suffered, He did not threaten, but committed Himself to Him who judges righteously; who Himself bore our sins in His own body on the tree, that we, having died to sins, might live for righteousness – by whose stripes you were healed" (I Pet. 2:21-24).

Last one: "Finally, all of you be of one mind, having compassion for one another; love as brothers, be tenderhearted, be courteous; not returning evil for evil or reviling for reviling, but on the contrary blessing, knowing that you were called to this, that you may inherit a blessing. For 'He who would love life And see good days, Let him refrain his tongue from evil, And his lips from speaking deceit. Let him turn away from evil and do good; Let him seek peace and pursue it. For the eyes of the Lord are on the righteous, And His ears are open to their prayers; But the face of the Lord is against those who do evil" (I Pet. 3:8-12).

As I read these verses for myself back-to-back, the once-fuzzy picture has started to finally come into sharp focus for me. I continue to fight within myself over definitions for "hate" and "dislike," but it has become painfully obvious to me that as a follower of the Lord Jesus I am expected to fiercely resist the temptation to bathe in the fleeting satisfaction of doing, speaking, or even wishing ill against my enemy. I don't mind telling you that that is a really tall order for me!

In Heb. 4:15, Jesus is described as our great High Priest who can sympathize with us because He was tempted in every imaginable way, but He remained perfectly sinless. The Bible doesn't say it in so many words, but I get the feeling that my Lord was hounded almost relentlessly by the devil. (Read Luke 4:1-13 and you'll see not only several specific temptations Satan leveled at Him, but also you will read that the Adversary only left Jesus temporarily. Satan would return, I'm guessing many times, to buffet the Son of God with one enticement after another.) Do you know when you get relief from temptation? When you yield to it! Jesus was tempted over and over again, but He never gave in, not even once.

As we continue to race toward the end of the Church Age, people (particularly those who are lost) are going to get more and more difficult to deal with (II Tim. 3:1-5). You read above, in I Cor. 4:13, that "...we have been made as the filth of the world, the offscouring of all things until now." The Wuest translation of the New Testament words it this way: "We have become in the estimation of the world as the filth discarded by humanity as the result of cleansing one's self, dirt scraped off of all things, to this very moment.[1]

Having lived my entire life in Christian America, I've never known what it was like to have the world regard the followers of Christ as scum. But the Christians who lived in Paul's day didn't know anything else. They were esteemed by their unsaved counterparts as no better than the refuse that is scrubbed off of grimy, nasty bodies in the bathtub after a long and sweaty day's work. Don't look now, but that is the very description of how the world around us is beginning to view you and me. I only *thought* that it's been hard to avoid hating people. Truth is, we ain't seen nothin' yet.

The Bible teaches that we're not to embrace evil, but we must love our enemy. One of the most practical ways for me to accomplish this is to remember that every Christian – myself included – was once an enemy of God (cf. Eph. 2:1-3). I need God's mercy no less than any other person who's ever lived, for I am no better. However, this fact doesn't translate into the incorrect view that I am supposed to be a doormat for the world. In Acts 22:28-29; 25:10-11, Paul used his Roman citizenship as leverage to ask for legal rights to which he was duly entitled. In both of these cases, Paul was the object of hatred and persecution by his own countrymen.

We see a similar illustration with Stephen in Acts 7:51-53, where he calls out the Jews for their wrongful opposition to God, and in vs. 54-58, they reacted by murdering him. In v. 60, as Stephen was dying, he prayed to the Lord that his persecutors would not be charged with their sin against him.

John the Baptist gives us another picture of how the Christian life should look when faced with resentment from the world. In Mark 6:17-20, Herod had John imprisoned (and ultimately beheaded – vs. 24-29) because John spoke boldly against Herod's sin.

Even the Lord Himself laid down such a pattern. Read the entire chapter of Matthew 23, and you'll see one long and stinging rebuke coming from the lips of our Creator. As it was with Stephen and John, Jesus was likewise murdered by His adversaries. All three men spoke the truth and all three paid for it with their lives. None of them retaliated against their foes. But they also never wavered or apologized for their having spoken out against evil.

Proverbs 31:8-9 instructs us: "Open your mouth for the speechless, In the cause of all who are appointed to die. Open your mouth, judge righteously, and plead the cause of the poor and needy." When we speak for righteousness, we quite literally speak for God. We are never to stay silent in the face of evil. As Paul wrote in II Cor. 5:20, "...we are ambassadors for Christ, as though God were pleading through us: we implore you on Christ's behalf, be reconciled to God." God reserves the right to take action against the things He hates, whereas you and I are to pray for our enemies, plead with them, and help them. (This is because, among other reasons, only God sees what's inside of a man. We can only know men by the fruit they bear.) To abhor evil (Rom. 12:9) is to stand fast in the face of it, being willing to accept whatever consequences may come of our objections but refusing to stay quiet. It means to warn people of the wrath that is to come if they persist in their sin.

Debbie, who can always be counted on to give me insights into the Scriptures that would never have occurred to me, has some things to say that I wish to add here. Her comments are a fitting conclusion to this chapter. She says that our job is to love our enemy, which means that we must do what we can to help them achieve their highest good. That always begins with helping them understand what God says about their sin. No matter what their response is, we must consistently keep ourselves separate from their evildoings, which is to say that we are never to affirm them in their actions but to advise them of the consequences. Below are some examples she gave of how this action plays out.

Noah tried to help others by warning them for 120 years while he built the ark. They rejected his counsel, so God separated Noah and his family from the rest of the world.

Lot tried to convince the men of Sodom not to do evil to his angelic guests. The townsmen disregarded his pleas, so God separated Lot and his family from the rest of the city.

Just ahead of Noah, Enoch tried to warn the people of their sin, but the people would not hear him. Because of his obedience, God separated Enoch from the earth before He judged it.

The disciples were to preach the good news to the world. If their hearers repudiated the love of the truth (II Thess. 2:10), Jesus' followers were to shake the dust off their feet as a witness against them. God separated His ambassadors from these wicked towns by sending them elsewhere, never to return that way again.

Today, Christians are called "haters" by the very people who truly hate God, those who reject the highest good found only in God's truth. (See Rom. 1:17, where Paul explains that the gospel itself reveals the righteousness of God.) What we're seeing today is the outworking of Isaiah 5:20-21: "Woe to those who call evil good, and good evil; Who put darkness for light, and light for darkness; Who put bitter for sweet, and sweet for bitter! Woe to those who are wise in their own eyes, And prudent in their own sight!"

Woe to them. Woe unto us all.

40

FREE AT LAST

There are many things I didn't discuss with you in this book. I never brought up evils like doctor-assisted suicide, the lies surrounding embryonic stem cell research, or the dirty secrets behind hospitals and organ donations. I could have curled your hair with one example after another of the social ills that go on all around us every day, but that would have served little purpose. My goal was to demonstrate that we are a people under divine judgment and what this truth means for us as Christians and Americans.

In this concluding chapter, I will leave you with some random observations and pointed recommendations. First, I have to burst a few bubbles about the late great United States. America is not going to recover from her present predicament. When I say that she is not going to recover, that means that she will *never* return to her former glory. Some of my prediction is an echo of what de Tocqueville said about America being great because of her being good (see Chapter 32).

But this forecast goes deeper than that. America did not become great because we worshiped false gods. America did not become great because we celebrated sexual degeneracy or because we butchered millions of unborn children under false pretenses. America became great because of our dependence upon the God of the Bible.

Furthermore, America was not a free nation because of Allah, or Vishnu, or Buddha, or Ahura Mazda. As I penned in numerous letters I sent to our governing authorities (such as those I published in the Appendices), America was free because Americans acknowledged the truth of the Bible to the exclusion of all opposing beliefs. We will not return to greatness because the Bible teaches that things in the times of the end will only get worse, not better.

Look at every other nation or people group throughout all of history. Was the Soviet Union great? Was it free? No, it was an oppressive, murderous, God-hating regime that ended when it collapsed upon itself. Very similar governments can be found in China, Cuba, Laos, North Korea, and Vietnam. The citizens of these countries have no rights of ownership, they have no freedom to speak their minds, they cannot protect themselves from an aggressive and zealous police state, and they most assuredly cannot practice the religion of their own choosing without dire repercussions.

As Americans, we've been accustomed to enjoying all of these freedoms, and it's because, as our Declaration of Independence rightly proclaims, "We hold these truths to be self-evident, that all men are created equal, that they are endowed by their Creator with certain unalienable rights, that among these are life, liberty and the pursuit of happiness. That to secure these rights, governments are instituted among men, deriving their just powers from the consent of the governed. That whenever any form of government becomes destructive of these ends, it is the right of the people to alter or to abolish it, and to institute new government, laying its foundation on such principles and organizing its powers in such form, as to them shall seem most likely to effect their safety and happiness."

One of several major reasons why America will never ascend to heights of years gone by is because Americans no longer believe that America was ever all that great. Everybody's busy trying to figure out how to revamp or even replace our Constitution, yet we fail to see that we're not following the one we have. God gave the world a great gift when He bestowed upon it this nation. God gave this nation a great gift when He gave us our Constitution and the small, limited government that was designed to be tightly bound by that same Constitution. No, I am not saying that any of our founding documents are on a par with the Word of God. There is but one Bible, one perfect Word. But our Constitution gave rise to the greatest nation in world history.

But Americans don't believe these things anymore. We have no fight left in us because we fail to see that the blanket of freedom our country once provided was something that was actually worth fighting to keep. Once again, please don't misunderstand me here. I am not saying that we shouldn't fight for our nation. On the contrary, I maintain that we should all do our part to participate in our government. Christians need to run for public office. Christians need to assemble and make their voices heard when debauchery rears its hideous head. It is our duty as citizens of both this country and of heaven (Rom. 13:1-7; Phil. 3:20) to give our all in the cause of righteousness, both for the sake of the coming Kingdom as well as for this earthly realm.

However, I am also warning you that you should not anticipate being successful in holding back the floodwaters of God's judgment forever. I repeat: God does not call us to be "successful;" He calls us to be obedient.

It shouldn't catch anyone off guard to hear that those who don't love the Lord have no appetite for His return to this world. Throughout the nearly 33 years before God saved me, I can assure you that I gave absolutely no thought to the preposterous concept that Jesus was coming again. Heck, I gave no thought to His having come the first time. But ever since March 28, 1997, the day He raised me from death to life, nary a day has passed where I didn't pause at least once or twice to consider the possibility that this might be the day my Savior will come to rapture His loved ones into glory. (For a detailed account of what the Bible says about the Rapture, read my first book.)

However, I have found there to be a disturbing trend in recent years, that being that many *Christians* no longer seem interested in doctrines pertaining to the end times. Perhaps everyone is preoccupied with paying the mortgage, keeping their spouse happy, finding a better job, raising the kids. Speaking of children, I've often heard it said that every time a baby is born, the child is proof that God wants the world to continue on. That may be a delightful sentiment, but it has no foundation in the truth. Reflect on these words from Jesus: "And as it was in the days of Noah, so it will be also in the days of the Son of Man: They ate, they drank, they married wives, they were given in marriage, until the day that Noah entered the ark, and the flood came and destroyed them all. Likewise as it was also in the days of Lot: They ate, they drank, they bought, they sold, they planted, they built; but on the day that Lot went out of Sodom it rained fire and brimstone from heaven and destroyed them all. Even so will it be in the day when the Son of Man is revealed" (Luke 17:26-30).

The birth of a child is an important event. That's why so much of this book is dedicated to the sacredness of human life and the enormity of the sin of abortion. But nothing – and I do mean NOTHING – compares to the magnitude of the coming of our Lord. Can I tell you a little secret? God isn't waiting for your grandbabies to grow up and graduate high school before He sends His Son back to this earth. He's not waiting on your best friend to get saved. He's not waiting on your nuptials so you can enjoy your honeymoon. God and His plans are much bigger and way more important than all of everything and everyone put together and whatever puny little milestones we may think we want to see come to pass. As Paul tells us in Rom. 11:36, "For of Him and through Him and to Him are all things, to whom be glory forever. Amen."

One of the chief problems that Lamech had was that he failed to see just how small he was and just how big God is. Lamech had no lasting posterity, and as we have seen, he shall be lost forever in the fires of eternal doom. You and I must learn this greatest of all lessons from Lamech: God is big, we are not. One of the best ways for you to live triumphantly in these perilous times is to keep your life in proper perspective. Jesus promised us that He would return. One of every 25 verses in the New Testament deals with His Second Coming. If He's coming back (and He is), why can't it be today?

Another problem with Lamech is that, left unchecked, he'll produce more Lamechs. Bible teacher Steve Farrar says that if you're a Christian, you're a leader. Whether you know it or not, people are constantly watching you. In Ezekiel 33:1-9, God gave His prophet a solemn task. Ezekiel was told that he was to be a "watchman" over the children of Israel. God exhorted Ezekiel to warn the people that they were in sin and rebellion against the Lord, and that they must repent immediately. If Ezekiel failed to perform this duty, the people would die in their sin, but the man of God would be held accountable for neglecting his errand. However, if he did as he was told and he sounded the alarm to his fellow citizens, then no matter what happened to them Ezekiel was off the hook.

Read the passage in Ezekiel, and then read II Cor. 5:10-11. Just as God called His spokesmen in the OT to shepherd the people back to righteousness, we have likewise been chosen to do the same with our contemporaries. How dedicated we are will have a direct impact on how things go for us at the Judgment Seat of Christ. No one listened to Noah, and none outside his family were saved. Lot was unable to persuade the lustful men of Sodom, and they were all destroyed along with the rest of the city. Do not worry about how many people you are able to rescue. Remember, you cannot make people listen; you can only make them hear.

Read II Thess. 2:1-4. This sobering passage peels back the curtain on the Last Days, as Paul touches on subjects like the Rapture, the revealing of the man Antichrist, and the seven-year Tribulation. In v. 3, we are given a hint about what we should be looking for just prior to the Day of the Lord, what Scripture calls the "falling away." As the storm clouds of judgment continue to gather, I see now that this falling away, or apostasy (which is the Greek word used here and is sometimes translated as "rebellion") is more far-reaching than I ever imagined. This brings me to my next point. What if the judgment of Romans 1 isn't about a single nation or people group? What if Romans 1 is part of a judgment on the entire world? What if this is just a warm-up for the global judgment to come, the Tribulation? If that's true (and I have every reason to believe it could be), then time is very short indeed. Act swiftly! Be urged on in your witnessing to your lost family members and friends! You don't know when the Lord may come and take you home, leaving them here to be swept away by the wrath of the Lamb.

Hang in there, friend. I know this book has been a bit of a downer at times, but you don't have far to go. One of the essential tools I want to deposit into your pack is a passion to keep unspotted by the world (James 1:27). God commands all believers to love neither the world nor the things in the world, for friendship with the world is hostility toward God (cf. Rom. 8:5-9; II Cor. 6:14-18; James 4:4; I John 2:15). Nowhere is the penalty from having been ensnared by such a sin more succinctly defined than in Romans 1:32, and nowhere is it more brilliantly demonstrated how it is to be avoided than in Daniel 1.

Please go to the book of Daniel right now, and read the entire first chapter. In vs. 1-2, Babylon came against Jerusalem and prevailed against it. In v. 3, King Nebuchadnezzar ordered that some of the Jews be taken into captivity and trained (insert the word "brainwashed" here) to serve in the king's court. In vs. 4-7, the outline of this indoctrination is given in three parts: the captives were to be trained in the ways of the Babylonian culture, they were given Babylonian names, and they were fed Babylonian food.

Now look at v. 8. Daniel raised no objection when he was subjected to a secular education. He didn't make a peep when he was given a silly new name. (Let's face it: Daniel is a much cooler name than Belteshazzar.) But the young man drew the line when he was told he had to dine on the delicacies of his new home and forsake the menu that he'd grown up on. Why? Because there are no scriptural prohibitions against going to public school, and there is nothing forbidding the changing of one's name. (Even God Himself changed names. He changed Abram to Abraham, Sarai to Sarah, Jacob to Israel, Saul to Paul, and Simon to Peter.)

However, God had strict guidelines about what was and was not considered food for His chosen people. Daniel drew the line in the same place where God did. This is the lesson Lamech never learned. He didn't have the written Word of God, but he had the testimony of his ancestors in addition to the fact that every single person on the planet had only one spouse.

You and I must learn the lesson of Lamech by following the example of Daniel. We <u>cannot</u> approve of the idolatry, sexual sin, or violence that has so saturated our world today, because God goes to great lengths throughout His Word to tell us that they are impermissible at all times and under all conditions. This is the warning of Romans 1:32.

It makes no difference if the whole world embraces these atrocities; we never can, not even by our silence. God is using these very sins to judge the world. How, then, can we participate, knowing where it's all leading?

Man has built into his DNA a desperate need to worship. We can't help it; we simply must give obeisance to someone or something. One reason for this is because God deserves our worship, and man is at his very best when we recognize God for who He is and He is given all honor and glory by His creatures who willingly submit themselves to His sovereignty. When actor/comedian Jamie Foxx called Barack Obama our "Lord and Savior," he was doing what people do: he was worshiping. He was engaging in a blasphemous act of worship, to be sure, but it was worship nonetheless.[1] It's not a question of whether or not you and I will worship. The question is, "Who (or what) is the object of our worship?" Only the God of the Bible is worthy! Only His precious Son Jesus is worthy!

At the beginning of this book, I gave you a few pithy maxims to consider as you read. My namesake, Teddy Roosevelt, was famous for living by the creed "Do hard things." The only thing harder than being a Christian is being a Christian in a society that wants to rid itself of God and the people who love Him. It's time for the body of Christ in America to get its fingernails dirty. There will be no avoiding it. You can't wish the old America to come back; it isn't going to. The country you once loved and would have died for is gone. We must now turn our attention away from what we once had, and we're to redirect our focus on the coming of the Lord. As it says in Hebrews 9:27-28: "And as it is appointed for men to die once, but after this the judgment, so Christ was offered once to bear the sins of many. To those who eagerly wait for Him He will appear a second time, apart from sin, for salvation."

I once heard someone say that a friend is someone who's going in when everyone else is coming out. I like that definition. It takes a person of stature and courage to stand up to the world and say, "You are my friend. I care enough about you to tell you the truth, regardless of the cost to me." There is no question that for today's Christian in western civilization, the stakes have gone up. Are you willing to come alongside a confused, combative friend and tell him things you know he needs to hear, no matter the consequences to you? It won't be easy, but with God's grace, it can be done. Just ask Daniel. Ask Noah. Ask Paul and the other apostles. Ask Jesus. If it were possible, ask Lamech.

“You may choose to look the other way but you can never say again that you did not know” – William Wilberforce.

“Therefore take up the whole armor of God, that you may be able to withstand in the evil day, and having done all, to stand” – Ephesians 6:13

APPENDIX A

Subject: Re: Muslim prayers on the House floor
From: TED MERRITT
Date: 1/7/2015 2:32 PM
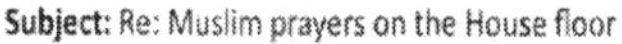

To Senator Lankford:

I want to begin by offering congratulations on your having been elected to the US Senate. I know you're busy getting settled into your new position, so I'll be brief. I started to write to you about a Muslim imam that was brought before Congress on Nov. 15, 2014 to open with a prayer to Allah. He was introduced by Speaker Boehner. However, in searching on the internet for the right YouTube video, I came across another instance where this exact same act occurred more than a year earlier. On July 31, 2013, the same thing happened. So now, instead of contacting you about only one occurrence, I'm writing to you about these two occasions. Here are the links to both events:

https://www.youtube.com/watch?v=P_z01cBnLbo

https://www.youtube.com/watch?v=RJC1spjgOHM

Senator, I have some very serious questions about this. First, were you in attendance for either of these two events? If you were, what did you do in response? If you weren't present, why not? Second, this is becoming a highly disturbing trend. Just exactly how many times has Congress called upon a Muslim cleric to pray to a nonexistent god, and what has been done about it? Third, why did your Oklahoma staffers not know anything about this? Did you not even tell them about these awful things? Finally, what (if anything) do you intend to do about this in the future? The oath of office for the congressional delegation goes something like this:

"I do solemnly swear (or affirm) that I will support and defend the Constitution of the United States against all enemies, foreign and domestic; that I will bear true faith and allegiance to the same; that I take this obligation freely, without any mental reservation or purpose of evasion; and that I will well and faithfully discharge the duties of the office on which I am about to enter: So help me God."

Allah is NOT God. Muslims are NOT Christians. Unlike the multitude of Bible verses and scriptural references (e.g. the Decalogue on the doors of the Supreme Court) that can be found all over the monuments and buildings on Capitol Hill, not one single "scripture" from the Qur'an can be found anywhere on any building in Washington. We ARE a Christian nation, no matter what Obama or anyone else says. Mr. Lankford, are you going to defend the Constitution against all enemies, both foreign and domestic? Will you bear true faith and

allegiance to the Constitution? Will you do these things, so help you God?

You have run your campaigns on the platform that you are a Christian. Consequently, you are now expected to discharge all of your duties as a Christian ought. Can you be counted on to do that?

Sincerely,

Ted Merritt

II Cor. 6:14-16

TOM COLE
4TH DISTRICT, OKLAHOMA

DEPUTY WHIP

COMMITTEE ON APPROPRIATIONS
LEGISLATIVE BRANCH - CHAIRMAN
DEFENSE
INTERIOR, ENVIRONMENT,
AND RELATED AGENCIES

COMMITTEE ON RULES

COMMITTEE ON THE BUDGET

Congress of the United States
House of Representatives

January 8, 2015

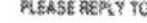
PLEASE REPLY TO:

☐ 2458 RAYBURN HOUSE OFFICE BUILDING
WASHINGTON, DC 20515
(202) 225-6165

☐ 2424 SPRINGER DRIVE
SUITE 201
NORMAN, OK 73069
(405) 329-6500

☐ 711 SW D AVENUE
SUITE 201
LAWTON, OK 73501
(580) 357-2131

☐ SUGG CLINIC OFFICE BUILDING
100 EAST 13TH STREET, SUITE 213
ADA, OK 74820
(580) 436-5375

Mr. Ted G. Merritt, II

Dear Mr. Merritt:

Thank you for contacting me regarding Imam Hamad Chebli serving as the Guest Chaplain in the House of Representatives. I appreciate hearing from you on this matter.

As you may know, the House of Representatives opens each day of session with a prayer. Often this prayer is offered by the House Chaplain, but is sometimes given by a guest chaplain, who is recommended to the Chaplain by a member of the House. On November 13, 2014 Representative Rush Holt (D-NJ) sponsored Imam Hamad Chebli to be the Guest Chaplain and to give the opening prayer. He is the seventh Imam to serve in the role of Guest Chaplain.

The First Amendment to the Constitution declares that "Congress shall make no law respecting an establishment of religion, or prohibiting the free exercise thereof." The protection of religious freedom at the core of our nation allows the practice of all religions even those we may not agree with. The House Chaplain welcomes chaplains of all faiths.

Again, thank you for contacting me. I always appreciate hearing from my fellow Oklahomans. Your input helps me do a better job representing the people of the Fourth District of Oklahoma. If I may ever be of any assistance to either you or your family, please do not hesitate to contact me. I also encourage you to visit my website at www.house.gov/coleto keep up with what is happening in Congress, and to learn more about the services my office can provide to the citizens of Oklahoma.

Sincerely,

Tom Cole
Member of Congress

March 12, 2015

Senator James Lankford
B40C Dirksen Senate Office Building
Washington, DC 20510

Dear Senator Lankford:

I contacted you by e-mail back in January, and I asked you to respond to some questions I was having about people from other religions who've been coming into the House chamber and opening sessions of Congress by praying to their preferred deity. It turns out that John Boehner has introduced a Muslim Imam to come and pray on at least a couple of occasions; I put the YouTube video links to those events in my e-mail.

Instead of getting a reply from you, though, I got a letter from Congressman Tom Cole. If I had wanted a response from Congressman Cole, I would have written to him and not you. But Mr. Cole, to the best of my knowledge, has never run his campaign on a Christian platform. You, on the other hand, have made much of your Christianity and your work in the ministry throughout your campaigns for the seats you've won in both the House and the Senate. That's why I wrote to you. I am your constituent, and I need to know if you can be trusted to behave like the man of God you claim to be.

I have included copies of both my original e-mail to you and the reply I received from Congressman Cole. It was a dishonorable thing you did when you handed the ball off to Mr. Cole. I am therefore appealing to you a second time, because I need to hear from you what you intend to do about these blasphemous and traitorous acts. As I pointed out in my e-mail, to have a person come and plead for the blessing of anyone other than Almighty God upon the proceedings of America's political business is an act of treason against both America and God.

We are a Christian nation, even though we no longer behave like it. My father fought in WWII, and my stepson was wounded while serving in Iraq. They did not risk their lives so the rest of us could live in a godless cesspool. In I Kings 18, Elijah challenged the prophets of Baal to a sacrificing tournament (I know you know the story!). In v. 21, an exasperated Elijah asked the people, "How long will you falter between two opinions? If the Lord is God, follow Him; but if Baal, follow him." Either our God is God or some other god is god. I don't expect Mr. Cole to know the answer to this query, but you have no excuse.

You've had multiple opportunities to do what's right about Obama and impeach him for any one of a host of crimes. His repeated lies about things like Obamacare and his thoughts on homosexual "marriage", Benghazi, Jonathan Gruber, Bowe Bergdahl, Hillary Clinton's lies and cover-ups, fast-and-furious, and the VA, IRS (Lois Lerner), and NSA (Edward Snowden) scandals all come immediately to mind. (Oh, and then there's the matter of the wholesale slaughter of the unborn, which Obama has taken to a whole new level.) He has made a mockery of our Constitution and our 3-branch system of government. When you stand before the Judgment Seat, do you suppose you might be asked what you did to prevent an illegal president from destroying the country you swore to defend and preserve? If so, what answer do you intend to give the King of kings?

My questions to you remain unanswered. Were you in the House chamber when, on at least two separate occasions, an enemy of God came and called upon a nonexistent divinity to bless Congress and our nation at the start of those sessions? If you were, what did you do to stop it? If you weren't there, why not? Why did you not tell your own staff about these atrocities? And what will you do to prevent these kinds of wicked acts in the future?

Maybe you don't remember an act of terrorism that occurred in Oklahoma about six months ago at the hands of a Muslim terrorist. In the town of Moore, less than 10 miles from my house, an employee of Vaughn Foods was viciously attacked and brutally killed by a Muslim man who sawed her head from her body. A week later, while her funeral was taking place, one David Myers of the Department of Homeland Security was dispatched by Obama to the Islamic Society of Greater Oklahoma City, where he extended the following greeting on behalf of Obama himself: "Michelle and I would like to extend our best wishes to Muslims in the United States and around the world who are celebrating Eid al-Adha, and to congratulate those performing the Hajj this year. On Eid, Muslims continue the tradition of donating to the poor and joining efforts with other faith communities in providing assistance to those suffering from hunger, sickness, oppression, and conflict. Their service is a powerful example of the shared roots of the world's Abrahamic faiths and how our communities can come together in shared peace, with dignity and a sense of justice." Alton Nolen, the butcher that massacred a defenseless woman, had direct ties to the organization that Obama's emissary was addressing. To be clear, Obama sent a man at taxpayer expense from Washington, D.C. to Oklahoma City to congratulate Muslims for their acts of charity, but he sent no one to a woman's funeral that was held only a few short miles away in Moore, and both events (the funeral and the president's greeting to the Muslims) took place on the very same day.

In the letter that should have come from you, Mr. Cole states that the Imam who opened Congress with his so-called prayer on Nov. 13, 2014 was the seventh Muslim cleric to fill the role of guest chaplain. Cole then goes on to misuse the First Amendment, writing that "the protection of religious freedom at the core of our nation allows the practice of all religions even those we may not agree with." Mr. Lankford, I challenge you to name for me one single nation that offers the religious freedom that America has historically given us that is NOT a primarily Christian nation. The only reason that Americans have enjoyed the right to worship however they choose is because of the fact that the Lord has always been our God. Once we've succeeded in completely expelling Him from our society, we will put in His place a tyrannical god, like those found in all Communist and Middle Eastern dictatorships. When that happens, there will be no freedoms (religious or otherwise) left for the people to enjoy. My wife also pointed out that if you allow Communism to take over you'll be without a job (no need for Senators, right?), but if you allow Islam to take control your very life would be in jeopardy (since you profess to be a Christian). No despotic regime has ever been sympathetic toward Christianity any more than it has cared to elect its leaders.

On Election Day in 2008, after the presidential results came in, my wife and I each made a prediction. She anticipated that our nation would abandon our Christian heritage and turn to Islam, and I said that we would never have another president, that Obama would be made "king." People used to laugh when we gave them our forecasts, but no one's laughing anymore. You're not so young, Mr. Lankford, that you don't remember what America was like when it was still great. And now, God has given you an opportunity to help facilitate the one thing we must do as a people if we're going to survive: we must repent of our sins.

Either you're a Christian or you're not. Will you stand up for truth and your sworn oath to defend the Constitution, or will you falter between two opinions? I can think of no greater act of blasphemy and treason than going along with a congressionally sanctioned so-called prayer of someone who doesn't even represent the Christian faith, the official religion of these United States. You've had many chances to be a statesman, worthy of the title and responsibility you've been given by the people you serve. Will you rise to that level, or will you be content to be just another politician, just another coward?

'Till He Comes,

Ted Merritt

enclosures

Rev. 3:15-16

APPENDIX B

August 3, 2015

U.S. House of Representatives
Committee on the Judiciary
2138 Rayburn HOB
Washington, D.C. 20515

To the U.S. House Judiciary Committee:

My name is Ted Merritt, and I live in Oklahoma City. Around the first of July, I contacted all of Oklahoma's congressional delegation in hopes of meeting with them (or someone from their staff) about the recent Supreme Court ruling over homosexual "marriage." I received a couple of phone calls from our senators and a letter from my congressman, but it appears that none of them are able to do very much about the decision. Since this is a matter involving the Supreme Court, I thought it would be appropriate to contact you about it. I know that no one on this committee represents me directly, but anything you could do to help America in this particular fight for its survival would be deeply appreciated. Please know that I want to be of assistance in any way that I can, so call or e-mail me at your convenience and let me know how I might be able to help. Many thanks! I'm sending you a copy of the letter I sent to Oklahoma's congressmen and senators in order to give you an idea of what I intend to accomplish. Here it is:

The Supreme Court's ruling over marriage last Friday has caused a constitutional crisis that requires our immediate attention. Consequently, I am requesting a personal meeting with all of Oklahoma's congressional delegation with the hope that we can devise a plan to correct this perversion of U.S. constitutional law. (It has been suggested that Congress can use Article I, Section 9 of the Constitution to prevent the enforcement of the ruling.) Below are several constitutional violations that I've found so far in my research of this legal aberration.

First, I wish to make reference to existing "hate crimes" legislation, as this decision will have a direct impact on how hate crimes are prosecuted. 18 U.S. Code Sec. 249, which was passed in 1969, covers "offenses involving actual or perceived race, color, religion, or national origin." In 2009, H.R. 1913 was enacted, which extends so-called hate crime protections to individuals with "actual or perceived gender, sexual orientation, gender identity, or disability" related issues.

With respect to the addendum passed in 2009, this law in itself runs headlong into the problem of mutual exclusivity. The First Amendment to the Constitution reads: "Congress shall make no law respecting an establishment of religion, or prohibiting the free exercise thereof; or abridging the freedom of speech, or of the press; or the right of the people peaceably to assemble, and to petition the government for a redress of grievances." First Amendment freedoms can either be enjoyed by the people who support homosexual unions or by those who oppose them, but not both. Since biblical Christianity does not allow for the recognition of homosexual "marriage" as a viable institution, they must inherently forfeit their right to the free exercise of their religion. It is important to note that this will directly and adversely affect other religious groups as well, such as Islam, since they, too, oppose homosexuality. Is the federal government prepared to deny this right to Christians, Muslims, and any other group whose beliefs and consciences prevent them from accepting this lifestyle?

Our freedom of speech will also be hampered by the Court's decision. As an example, my wife and I own two cars; both vehicles display a bumper sticker that reads: "Marriage: One Man One Woman." Since homosexuals have been given the right to "marry," it must be assumed that religious freedom will have to be surrendered in order for such groups to stay in accordance with the law. That being the case, does that mean that the people will be stripped of their freedom of speech as well? We are all aware of the bakers and photographers and wedding chapels that have been targeted by the homosexual lobby and vilified in the courts over the past few years; this ruling will only exacerbate the wrongs that will be done to people with moral and religious objections to this kind of sexual misconduct.

Another freedom that will be quashed is the freedom of the press. Radio, television, film, and internet programs that are of a religious or moral nature will not be allowed to voice their disapproval of sexual perversion. The same will be true for people who wish to peaceably assemble, whether in a house of worship or in an open public setting. In late 2013, a traveling theater production came to the Civic Center in Oklahoma City. Titled "The Most Fabulous Story Ever Told," it was a vile and blasphemous play that ostensibly told "Bible stories" from a homosexual perspective. The play included simulated acts of homosexuality and even bestiality, and it blatantly mocked the Christian faith. On opening night of that production, a group of concerned citizens came out to peacefully pray, witness, and yes, protest the play. Under the Court's ruling, we can be sure that such gatherings will be criminalized.

Until 1962, every state in the Union had laws that made sodomy a felony crime. What has changed since then that makes this abominable lifestyle worthy of the people's forced acceptance? What's to become of the people who take offense to homosexuality? How will they be able to teach their young, innocent children that what the courts, the media, and the public schools are telling them is propaganda, lies, and filth? To borrow from the homosexual lobby, who says that they only want to be free to love whomever they choose, what if the one you love happens to be Jesus?

I'm certain that this judicial action will have many more devastating effects on our society. The homosexual lifestyle carries with it a variety of other social ills, including drug and alcohol abuse, venereal disease and other serious health problems, violence, rape, pornography, and child molestation, abuse, and exploitation.

Finally, Article III, Section 1 of the U.S. Constitution states that Supreme Court justices "...shall hold their offices during good behavior..." With more than 60% of states having passed laws that recognize marriage as being strictly one man and one woman, how can the Court's annulment of these laws in utter disregard of the will of the people be considered "good behavior"?

Much more could be said, but I'll leave off with this one last thought. If marriage can be between two men or two women, what is to stop it from being between more than two people? What will keep it from being between a 35-year-old adult and a 6-year-old child? What about a person and an animal, or a person and an inanimate object? If marriage can mean anything, then marriage ultimately means nothing. If it means nothing, the family is destroyed. The family is by far the most important institution on this earth. If the family is destroyed, the society is destroyed. I implore you, Congressman, to contact me at once. It is my earnest desire that I meet with you and the other congressional delegates from Oklahoma as soon as possible in order that we might discuss how we can successfully combat this attempt to annihilate our nation and enslave its people.

Many Thanks,

Ted Merritt

BIBLIOGRAPHY

Unless otherwise indicated, Scripture quotations are taken from the THE NEW KING JAMES VERSION. Copyright 1982 by Thomas Nelson, Inc. Used by permission.

Chapter 6: Goin' Green with Gore

1. Steven Goddard's *Real* Science, stevengoddard.wordpress.com/1970s-ice-age-scare/, accessed March, 2015.
2. Ibid.
3. Ibid.
4. Ibid.
5. ("Gore Defends Mansion's Power Consumption," CBS News online, http://www.cbsnews.com/news/gore-defends-mansions-power-consumption/

Chapter 7: I Know Whom I Have Believed

1. The peacock spider is a real spider. For fun, look up its mating ritual on YouTube at http://www.youtube.com/watch?v=d_yYC5r8xMI&feature=youtube_gdata_player. Accessed March, 2015.

Chapter 8: Greater Than a Wombat

1. Noah Webster, "American Dictionary of the English Language," San Francisco, pub. 1967 by Foundation for American Christian Education, reprint of original publication in 1828.

2. Ibid.

Chapter 10: Georgia (Guidestones) on My Mind

1. Georgia Guidestones, Wikipedia, http://en.m.wikipedia.org/wiki/Georgia_Guidestones, accessed March, 2015.

Chapter 11: If You Can't Beat Them, Shut 'em Up

1. "New Inquisition: Punish Climate-Change 'Deniers,'" World Net Daily, article available online at http://www.wnd.com/2015/03/new-inquisition-punish-climate-change-deniers/. Article accessed online April, 2015.

Chapter 12: What is Truth?

1. "Barack Obama: 'Sin is Being Out of Alignment with My Values,'" Godfather Politics, article online at http://godfatherpolitics.com/4096/barack-obama-sin-is-being-out-of-alignment-with-my-values/. Accessed May, 2015.

2. Noah Webster, American Dictionary of the English Language, San Francisco, pub. 1967 by Foundation for American Christian Education, reprint of original publication in 1828.

Chapter 13: Two Wives, One Home

1. See the ruling of Engel v. Vitale, decided June 25, 1962. Summary of ruling available online at http://www.nationalcenter.org/cc7252.htm.

2. "Hugo Black's Wall of Separation of Church and State," Garland Goff, Liberty University website, http://digitalcommons.liberty.edu/honors/315/. Accessed May, 2015.

Chapter 14: In the Church as it is at Home

1. David Jeremiah, "The Jeremiah Study Bible," USA, Worthy Publishing, 2013, pg. 1592.

Chapter 15: Ladies First

1. David Jeremiah, "The Jeremiah Study Bible," USA, Worthy Publishing, 2013, pg. 466.

Chapter 17: The New Normal

1. Noah Webster, American Dictionary of the English Language, San Francisco, pub. 1967 by Foundation for American Christian Education, reprint of original publication in 1828.

2. ("Rainbow Flag (LGBT movement)," Wikipedia, accessed May 2015, http://en.m.wikipedia.org/wiki/Rainbow_flag_(LGBT_movement).

Chapter 18: The Caboose of a Long Train

1. "A 'Father' Will Marry His 'Son' in Pennsylvania – But It's Not What You Think," Inquisitr, online article posted 5/21/15 at http://www.inquisitr.com/2107395/a-father-will-marry-his-son-in-pennsylvania-but-its-not-what-you-think/.

2. "Nadine Schweigert, North Dakota Woman, 'Marries Herself,' Opens Up About Self-Marriage," Huffington Post, May 25, 2012. Article online at http://www.huffingtonpost.com/2012/05/25/nadine-schweigert-woman-marries-herself_n_1546024.html.

Chapter 19: Hollow Arguments

1. "'Queen James Bible'" Clumsily Cleanses Scriptures of "'Homophobia,'" The New American, article posted online on December 24, 2012. Accessed online in June, 2015 at http://www.thenewamerican.com/culture/faith-and-morals/item/14025-%E2%80%9Cqueen-james-bible%E2%80%9D-clumsily-cleanses-scriptures-of-%E2%80%9Chomophobia%E2%80%9D.

2. "I'm Gay. And I Want My Kid to Be Gay, Too," Washington Post, Feb. 20, 2015, article online at http://www.washingtonpost.com/opinions/im-gay-i-want-my-kid-to-be-gay-too/2015/02/19/eba697c2-b847-11e4-aa05-1ce81263fdd2_story.html.

Chapter 20: Demanding Our Holiness

1. John MacArthur, The MacArthur Study Bible (NKJV) Nashville, Word Publishing, 1997), pg. 1927.

Chapter 22: An Introduction to a Culture of Death

1. "Political Party Platforms," The American Presidency Project, article posted online on Sept. 3, 2012 at http://www.presidency.ucsb.edu/ws/?pid=101962.

Chapter 23: Booing God, Hailing Satan

1. YouTube video, accessed June, 2015 at http://youtu.be/aG6qgSfaARE.

2. Ibid.

3. Ibid.

4. "Wendy Davis' Stunning Filibuster of a Texas Abortion Bill," The Week, article written by Peter Weber and posted online at http://theweek.com/articles/462815/wendy-davis-

stunning-filibuster-texas-abortion-bill. Article accessed June, 2015.

5. YouTube video, accessed June, 2015 at http://youtu.be/1OApEt72GGM.

6. YouTube video, accessed June, 2015 at http://youtu.be/pKrfCow6Lyk.

Chapter 24: Killers on the Loose

1. “Political Party Platforms,” The American Presidency Project, article posted online on Sept. 3, 2012 at http://www.presidency.ucsb.edu/ws/?pid=101962.

2. CNN reporting at Johnstown, Pa. Statements made to a live audience. YouTube video, accessed July, 2015 at http://youtu.be/A70M2AbnX5A.

3. Presidential campaign speech, made July 9, 2008 at a fundraiser for the Planned Parenthood Action Fund. YouTube video, accessed July, 2015 at http://youtu.be/pf0XIRZSTt8.

4. Speech given by Obama to Planned Parenthood National Conference on April 29, 2013. YouTube video, accessed July, 2015, at http://youtu.be/kUiB-2n2vPM.

5. Homepage of the Planned Parenthood Action Center, accessed July, 2015, at

http://www.plannedparenthoodaction.org/issues/abortion-access.

Chapter 25: Roe v. Life

1. "Roe v. Wade Supreme Court decision," article posted online at womenshistory.about.com. Jone Johnson Lewis, accessed July, 2015 at http://womenshistory.about.com/od/abortionuslegal/p/roe_v_wade.htm.
2. Ibid, emphasis theirs.
3. "Partial Birth Abortion," article posted on Abortion Facts website at http://www.abortionfacts.com/literature/partial-birth-abortion. Article accessed online July, 2015.
4. Ibid.
5. "Late-Term Abortionist Martin Haskell Allowed to Avoid Ohio Law," article by Steven Ertelt and posted online on October 4, 2011 at LifeNews.com. Article available online at http://www.lifenews.com/2011/10/04/late-term-abortionist-martin-haskell-allowed-to-avoid-ohio-law/. Accessed July, 2015.
6. "Judge Orders Late-Term Abortionist Martin Haskell to Close His Clinic," article by Steven Ertelt and posted online on August 15, 2014 at LifeNews.com. Article available online at

http://www.lifenews.com/2014/08/15/judge-orders-late-term-abortionist-martin-haskell-to-close-his-clinic/. Accessed July, 2015.

Chapter 26: From Hippocrates to Hypocrites

1. "Hippocratic Oath," Britannica online, article online at http://www.britannica.com/topic/Hippocratic-oath. Accessed July, 2015.

2. The Internet Classics Archive, The Oath by Hippocrates, article accessed online at http://classics.mit.edu/Hippocrates/hippooath.html. Article accessed September, 2015.

3. "The Hippocratic Oath Today," PBS online, article by Peter Tyson and posted online on March 27, 2001 at http://www.pbs.org/wgbh/nova/body/hippocratic-oath-today.html. Article accessed July, 2015.

4. "Mutilated Babies Storm into Presidential Race," article written by Garth Kant and posted online on World Net Daily's website on July 10, 2015. Article online at http://www.wnd.com/2015/07/huckabee-selling-unborn-body-parts-grotesque/. Accessed July, 2015.

5. Ibid.

6. Ibid.

Chapter 27: Facts Are Stubborn Things

1. Information provided by the Pro-Life Action League at http://prolifeaction.org/faq/abortion.php. Website accessed in July, 2015.

2. Information provided by whyprolife.com at http://www.whyprolife.com/planned-parenthood. Website accessed in July, 2015.

3. Ibid.

4. Here is a collection of some web addresses that can point you to scientific research and evidence of a direct link between abortion and risk of breast cancer: (a) http://www.naturalnews.com/034455_breast_cancer_Bibles_Planned_Parenthood.html; (b) http://www.texasrighttolife.com/a/520/Lets-Cure-Breast-Cancer-Not-Fund-Abortions#.VbBkPOo8Kru; (c) http://dailycaller.com/2010/10/12/komen-breast-cancer-charity-provides-funding-for-planned-parenthood/; (d) http://www.lifenews.com/2011/10/11/pink-ribbon-scdandal-pro-life-groups-speak-out-against-komen/.

Chapter 28: The Silent Witness

1. For information on this group, go to http://www.centerformedicalprogress.org/.

Chapter 29: The Written Witness

1. This information available online at the U.S. Abortion Clock. Go to http://www.numberofabortions.com/. This information was retrieved online in August, 2015.

2. Ibid.

3. Ibid.

Chapter 30: The Human Witness

1. "Kermit Gosnell," Wikipedia, accessed August, 2015 at https://en.m.wikipedia.org/wiki/Kermit_Gosnell.

2. "Bernard Nathanson," Wikipedia, accessed August, 2015 at https://en.m.wikipedia.org/wiki/Bernard_Nathanson.

3. "Bernard Nathanson, Abortion Provider Turned Pro-Life Activist, Dies," article by Emma Brown, The Washington Post, posted online February 22, 2011. Article accessed August, 2015 at http://voices.washingtonpost.com/postmortem/2011/02/bernard-nathanson-abortion-pro.html.

4. "Bernard Nathanson: 'I Was Shaken to the Roots of My Soul,'" online article by John Mallon, posted online at

http://www.johnmallon.net/Site/Bernard_Nathanson.html. Accessed August, 2015.

5. Ibid.

6. Ibid.

Chapter 32: A Call to Arms

1. "Quote taken from "Death of a Nation" by John Stormer, posted online at Great Christian Quotes.com. Accessed August, 2015 at http://greatchristianquotes.com/Quotes/Great%20because%20good.htm.

2. "The Pulpit is Responsible for It," online article written by Chuck Baldwin and posted April 13, 2013 on Renew America website. Article accessed August, 2015 at http://www.renewamerica.com/columns/baldwin/130413.

Chapter 33: What Little I Can Do, I Will Do

1. "U.S. House of Representatives LITERALLY Bow to Allah as Muslim Imam Delivers Prayer," posted November 15, 2014 on YouTube. Video accessed August, 2015 at http://youtu.be/lEnvtMpKGW0.

2. "Obama's Congress Opens with Muslim Imam's Prayer to Allah," recorded live on July 31, 2013 and posted August 7, 2013 on YouTube. Video

accessed August, 2015 at http://youtu.be/P_z01cBnLbo.

3. "Spiritual Heritage and Government Monuments," All About History, article posted online at http://www.allabouthistory.org/spiritual-heritage-and-government-monuments-faq.htm. Article accessed August, 2015.

Chapter 34: How badly Do You Want In?

1. "The Who Concert Disaster," Wikipedia, article accessed September, 2015 at https://en.m.wikipedia.org/wiki/The_Who_concert_disaster.

Chapter 37: A Godly Love

1. Quote obtained from the ESV Study Bible Notes electronic version, product available on the Olive Tree Bible Study App for Apple and Android brand devices. The ESV Study Bible is published by Crossway Publishing Company, Wheaton, IL. Published 2009. In book format, quote is on pg. 1250.

Chapter 38: Singing While They Scream

1. "Dietrich Bonhoeffer," Wikipedia, article accessed September, 2015 at https://en.m.wikipedia.org/wiki/Dietrich_Bonhoeffer#Abwehr_agent.

2. "George Tiller," Wikipedia, accessed September, 2015 at https://en.m.wikipedia.org/wiki/George_Tiller#Assassination_in_May_2009.

Chapter 39: Solving the Riddle

1. "The New Testament, An Expanded Translation," Kenneth Wuest, pg. 390, William B. Eerdmans Publishing Co., Grand Rapids, MI, 1961.

Chapter 40: Free at Last

1. https://www.youtube.com/watch?v=g-MYwUuidLo

4/13 Sharon

Made in the USA
Charleston, SC
25 November 2015